WEAR VINTAGE NOW!

For more information and updates, visit the author's blog:

denisebrain.com/vintage-denisebrain

WEAR VINTAGE NOW!

CHOOSE IT, CARE FOR IT, STYLE IT YOUR WAY

by
Margaret
Wilds

IngramSpark

Wear vintage and make the world brighter

— DENISEBRAIN

Top-drawer wearable women's vintage clothing, smiles, pink, french horn, and the occasional manatee — My story

I STARTED WEARING VINTAGE CLOTHING in 1974 because it was fashion I could afford with the pocket change of a teenager and the soul of a person who never quite felt like she fit in. I picked up my love of vintage early and have stuck with it through decades of changing styles.

After many years of stocking only my own closet with my vintage finds, I decided to turn it into a business, DENISEBRAIN. The year was 1999, and I started selling women's vintage clothing on eBay, then later on my own website and Etsy. Most of my business has been online, and I learned early the challenges of shopping the web for *any* clothes, but especially *vintage* clothes. The myriad styles, fabrics, and greatly varying descriptions from sellers make finding the right item a skilled pursuit. So I studied, read, asked questions, listened, and learned. I fueled my passion and worked to be the kind of seller I'd like to buy from.

Vintage isn't the only passion I pursue. My business name is based on Dennis Brain, one of the greatest horn players of all time. As a professional hornist, he has always been one of my heroes. Even though my name is Maggie, some people mistakenly call me Denise, but I really don't mind.

What else fuels my soul? I love all wild things, but most especially manatees. 10% of my sales go to Save the Manatee Club for the protection of this beloved endangered animal.

I care a lot about people trying to lift themselves up. 100% of the profits from sales in the Pink Heart Shop section of my Etsy store go to Dress for Success Worldwide, helping women thrive in work and in life.

Oh, and pink. I love pink. Not in a girly-girl way, but in a visceral, it-just-makes-me-happy way. My business branding is unabashedly pink, I write notes with a pink pen, and my vintage clothes? Lots of colors, but especially pink.

Enough about me, let's talk about you. I'm genuinely interested in how vintage can outfit you for the passions *you* pursue.

Who this book is for, and why

THIS BOOK IS FOR EVERYONE who loves wearing or collecting women's vintage clothing.

Whether you appreciate vintage for the style, the value, the quality, the fit, the fact that it's recycled and better for the planet, or the unique way it allows you to dress, I believe you will find vintage is worth any challenge it might present—and my hope is that this book will help make it a joy for you.

These days there are so many vintage items to be found online that the selection is astounding—you can actually get quite specific in your searches. Are you trying to find a 1960s emerald green chiffon party dress in a size XL? A 1950s *Lady and the Tramp*-print circle skirt in red? A 1970s Enid Collins Gemini handbag? I can remember when, before examples reached the eyes of so many through the internet, only a minuscule percentage of people would have known that such a dress, circle skirt, and handbag even existed. Now there are ardent fans and collectors of all sorts of vintage finery, and you can find both the items and the people online.

You can browse the fashion collections of museums and read about the history of designers and labels online. You can peruse the Instagram feeds and blogs of vintage wearers and see how they style their finds. You can participate in discussion forums and Facebook groups, connect with like-minded people across platforms, and pin your favorite finds on Pinterest—the accessibility is dazzling and dizzying. Plus, need I say, you can browse online while sitting on your couch with your dog at your side and a glass of wine in your hand?

Yet despite all the ease of online browsing and shopping, if you are fortunate enough to be near one, a brick-and-mortar vintage shop will give you the chance to try things on and assess them in person. Shop owners can also be great sources of inspiration and information. Some will search for items for you and keep you in mind when they find them. I love vintage stores and visit them when I can. You might want to too, if for no other reason than to help keep a small shop—one that adds charm and strength to its neighborhood—in business. The vintage fashion trade is peopled by small business owners, and you can support these online as well as in your town.

This book is designed to help answer some of the questions I've been asked most often about choosing, purchasing, and wearing vintage fashion. How do you decide on the size? What should you do if your vintage item doesn't quite fit? How do you take care of it? What vintage should you wear and how should you wear it?

I wrote this guide for vintage fashion newcomers—to offer them confidence and joy in their choices. But even though this book is taking it from the top, it also offers seasoned vintage fashionistas tips to fine-tune their skills.

My expertise is in women's vintage fashion, so although this book may include information that is also useful to someone interested in men's vintage (and to me there is nothing more stylish than a man wearing vintage well!), I lean heavily toward issues specific to women's clothing.

Although I hope to help answer questions and encourage thoughtful decisions, I am not going to tell you how to dress in, say, impeccable head-to-toe 1950s vintage. My aim is to help you discover your own style. In the past there were strict dos and don'ts—hem lengths, colors, heel heights, proportions—that everyone strove to adhere to. Now, many of us are lucky to have the latitude to dress in our own unique way, if not completely without constraints, at least with considerable freedom. Variety is one of the best things about vintage—it can give you the opportunity to express more of who you really are through the way you dress. It can help magnify the You of you.

Now that wearing vintage fashion is trendy, you'll find that in some places there is a social aspect to style, where people who identify with each other tend to dress similarly in their vintage fashions. Often hair and makeup are part of the look, and a great deal of effort goes into a highly polished appearance. That can be inspiring to some, but intimidating to many others. Don't let it be. It's never wrong to be a self-assured and stylish pack of one.

Who can wear vintage? I can't think of one single person who can't. You do not have to be part of the boho or rockabilly scenes. You don't have to have perfect red lipstick and victory rolls, false eyelashes and a Vidal Sassoon bob, finger waves and silk stockings. You don't have to be part of any scene, or belong to any club—but you can if you want to!

In the years since I began my vintage fashion business, I have had the privilege of hearing many customers' stories and learning just how varied vintage lovers really are. I've sold vintage to a girl of thirteen who wanted to experience what her great-grandmother had experienced, and to a woman in her eighties who wanted to relive an event from her youth. I had a customer who apologized for a late payment on a suit because she was working at the Pentagon on September 11, 2001 (I assured her I could hardly imagine how she remembered to pay at all and added a brooch to wear with the suit), and a customer who was thrilled to spot and purchase her own late mother's high school letter jacket from 1957. I have had loyal customers purchase full wardrobes from me and I have outfitted weddings and school plays. I have sold clothing to several Parisian designers, an Aztec princess who teaches elementary school, a mayor's wife, a mayor, actresses, museum curators, journalists, novelists, a policewoman, Broadway and television costumers, an opera singer, an indie musician, a famous rock star, a biologist, my neighbor, a skiing champion, a woman who uses a wheelchair, my best friend. These people are of all ages, sizes, styles, and walks of life.

There are so many stories—and part of the fun of vintage fashion *is* the stories, whether that's the history of a dress's label or style, the personal story from the original owner of a dress, or the story of the woman who then purchases the dress and starts a new chapter. It feels like holding hands across generations. Wouldn't you like to be part of this continuing history?

Of course you would. Let's get at it.

Vintage myth busting

MANY MYTHS PERSIST around the buying, selling, and wearing of vintage fashion, and some of these keep people from finding what they want, or even from exploring vintage in the first place. Do any of these myths sound familiar to you? We are going to debunk these, so stick around.

1. VINTAGE CLOTHES ARE TOO SMALL FOR ME

ABSOLUTELY NOT TRUE. Although there are more vintage items in XS, small, and medium sizes, there are plenty in larger sizes.

Try searching the vintage clothing on Etsy for sizes called XL or plus size; you might also try the popular terms "volup" and "curvy." Sellers will usually highlight an item in what would currently be considered a larger size with search terms such as these, based on a garment's measurements.

If you are plus size and have questions, you might find an answer (and inspiration) in the honest and positive writing and photos shown on the Va-Voom Vintage blog. You might start with her page "Plus Size Vintage Q&A."

All you need to know to get a comfortable, flattering fit is in "Figuring out vintage fit and size" on page 55.

2. YOU CAN FIND GREAT VINTAGE FOR CHEAP ANY TIME YOU WANT AT A THRIFT STORE.

IF YOU CAN, *would you mind sending me the address of said thrift*? If you love the thrill of the hunt, join the pack—you may find something you love. Just to be clear, thrift stores sell secondhand clothes that have been donated to them, often, at least in part, to raise funds for a charitable institution. In many places, thrift store vintage tends to be ordinary to lower quality from the '80s and newer—that's just the average of what is out there to be donated. You may live where there are great finds to be had here and there, but most are not so lucky. A vintage shop that, to varying degrees, has clothing curated by its owner, has done the hunting for you. Yes, it might cost more than a thrift store, but it will save you a tremendous amount of time and effort over thrift store shopping. Further, some thrift stores have become aware that they have something valuable when a vintage donation comes in, and their prices can equal or even exceed the prices of a vintage store.

To sharpen your eye for items of good quality and value, read "The vintage mindset" on page 27 and "Condition of vintage items: What to look for" on page 74.

3. Everything that is listed as *Mad Men* or *Downton Abbey* dates from the era portrayed in the shows.

BEWARE OF POPULAR KEYWORDS used to sell vintage items. I have seen 1980s dresses described as *Mad Men* or "flapper." Some popular keywords that I've seen used cavalierly: mod, hippie, Gatsby, Titanic. There are more–many more. If you are looking for a vibe and don't care when the item was actually made, then you may be fine picking out a sequined dress made in India in the '80s and wearing it as a flapper-style dress. In fact it may be the best choice among wearable clothes for the purpose. Just be informed so you don't pay authentic flapper dress prices!

Sourcing tips and search terms are included throughout the book to help you find the look you want.

4. I should look for vintage clothing in the same size I wear in modern clothing.

COURTESY OF REFUNKED JUNKIES

I'VE SEEN PEOPLE reject vintage size 14 items that would fit them perfectly because they were sure they would never wear a 14. Numbers are just numbers, and vintage numbers are particularly disconcerting to the modern mind. Focus on the item's measurements and compare them to your own.

The chapter "Figuring out vintage fit and size" (page 55) will get you past your fear of those vintage size numbers.

5. THE ORIGINAL PRICE TAG ON A VINTAGE ITEM INDICATES SOMETHING LIKE THE CURRENT VALUE.

NOPE. See "The vintage mindset" on page 27.

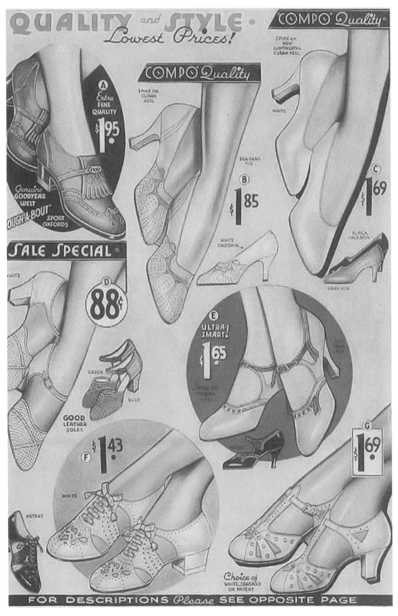

1933

6. Sears items from the 1950s are like Sears items now.

Sears, like many U.S. stores, once stocked clothing made in the U.S. almost exclusively. The quality, style, and construction surpassed what you will generally see today, even for what was considered day-to-day clothing. Vintage ordinary quality beats new ordinary quality, hands down.

For a more in-depth discussion of quality and value, see "The vintage mindset" on page 27.

70s HAT FROM VINTAGESTEW ON ETSY; 50s SWIMSUIT FROM GIBSON GIRL VINTAGE; ELLEN VERNIER OF TWO OLD BEANS VINTAGE / TWOOLDBEANS.ETSY.COM / @TWOOLDBEANS ON INSTAGRAM; 1946 DRESS ON MENA LAZAR—ALL VINTAGE ITEMS WITH SEARS LABELS

7. All used clothing is musty, dirty, smelly, etc.

Some is, much isn't. For those just getting started with vintage, it is a considerably better bet to purchase items in excellent condition and keep a sharp eye (and nose) out for damage. Online sellers should disclose any odors that they can detect in their vintage pieces. If a seller writes little about the condition of a piece you are interested in, don't hesitate to ask specifically about odors along with other issues.

Before you go shopping, read the chapter "Condition of vintage items: What to look for" (page 74). If you have your heart set on an item in less-than-stellar condition, or already own a piece in need of a little TLC, I share all my tips and tricks in "Taking care of your vintage finery" (page 79).

8. Vintage clothes look like costumes.

ONLY IF YOU WANT them to! Some people proudly dress in head-to-toe vintage as if they stepped out of, say, a 1954 *Vogue*–they don't care if others think it looks costume-y. And many, many others incorporate their vintage with considerable subtlety. It's all a matter for your taste. Take Sophia Zell, wearing her '70s vintage dress on Instagram @sophiazell, or Nora Thoeng in her '50s vintage dress and hat on her NoraFinds blog. On Instagram, as well as many personal style blogs, you can find lots of people incorporating vintage pieces into their unique styles.

Check out "How to wear vintage" on page 12.

COURTESY SOPHIA ZELL / COURTESY NORA THOENG

9. You should buy an authentic 1920s flapper dress to wear to a Roaring Twenties party.

THIS QUITE STUNNING AUTHENTIC 1920s beaded silk dress from Shrimpton Couture sold for (justifiably) $2,400. Even if it's in wonderful condition, with the weight of the beading on silk of this age, wearing this gorgeous dress would take the utmost care. I'd say the Charleston is out.

COURTESY SHRIMPTON COUTURE

Are you interested in acquiring older vintage or antique clothing? Vintage is usually defined as 20–100 years old, antique greater than a century old. This book focuses on wearable vintage, and if you are interested in wearing older vintage and antique clothing, please read my caveat on page 16 first.

10. The most valuable vintage items you might have in your closet (or your mother's and grandmother's closets) are wedding dresses and fur coats.

I'M VERY SORRY to say it, but the prices paid for these two categories of items wrongly set up the assumption that their value must be exceptionally great now. Wedding dresses are such a personal thing, and although there are beautiful exceptions, often a vintage wedding dress is not in a style that's classic enough, or it has stains or other frailties that make a woman not want it for her big day. I love to see wedding dresses passed down in a family, and furs as well. Vintage furs have many devotees, but furs can only be cleaned by furriers and they must be stored correctly. If not cared for, their condition deteriorates. There are also a number of fur types that came from animals that were previously allowed to be traded but are protected and prohibited from being sold today.

See one family's wedding dress, worn by brides for generations, on page 29.

11. WEAR WHAT MY GRANDMOTHER WORE? IT'S ALL SO FRUMPY!

OH YEAH?

JOHN W. MOSLEY PHOTOGRAPH COLLECTION, CHARLES L. BLOCKSON AFRO-AMERICAN COLLECTION, TEMPLE UNIVERSITY LIBRARIES, PHILADELPHIA, PA

12. You'll find an original Dior New Look suit, 1920s Chanel dress, or Westwood punk outfit at your local vintage shop if you ask nicely.

You can bring a box of chocolates *and* a million dollars, but the most desirable items will not materialize often. You will generally have more luck online, but expect such iconic items to be rare and extremely valuable.

13. This belonged to my mother's best friend's aunt and she had good taste so it must be valuable.

and

14. I just tossed three huge trash bags filled with my mother's '50s dresses; they're worthless, aren't they?

The extremes are often wrong: For the most part vintage (New Look Dior aside) is not worth its weight in gold, but it certainly has value. You can get a feel for many types of vintage fashion items' going rates at any given time by searching online. For instance, at the time of this writing, a search on Etsy for "1950s black cotton eyelet vintage dress" will bring back 49 results with a price range from $24 to $249. The median price is $85.

Have a look at "Quality and true value" on page 27.

15. If it has a side zipper…

…it is definitely from the '40s. If it has a nylon zipper, it is definitely '70s or newer. A crinoline slip in a skirt or dress means it is from the '50s. If it's beaded, it's flapper. If it has shoulder pads, it is from the '40s. If it has pinked seams, it has to be vintage.

There are ways to identify the vintage eras of items, but there are no blanket statements like these that hold true in every case. Look at "Quick

Tips for Dating Vintage" on the Vintage Fashion Guild site for some basics, but realize that it isn't a perfect science. For instance, metal zippers were used by home seamstresses long after they went out of use by manufacturers. Reproduction and vintage-inspired clothing can fool a newcomer to vintage.

16. EVERYTHING VINTAGE BELONGED TO DEAD PEOPLE.

OK, THIS ONE MAKES ME LAUGH, but it is a serious issue for some. If you truly feel squeamish at the thought of wearing something someone else wore, keep in mind that the new clothing you buy may also have been worn by someone else, in the dressing room or before being returned to the store.

Many a person has passed on whose clothing is perfectly wonderful. You honor them by keeping this facet of their history alive. Older women have told me they are very pleased to have their clothing worn by younger women around the world.

17. THIS BELONGED TO MY GREAT AUNT AND SHE SWORE IT WAS FROM THE 1920s, SO IT HAS TO BE.

IT IS AMAZING how many people remember with scientific clarity exactly when and where they purchased and wore certain items. Then there are those who don't.

18. IF IT DOES NOT HAVE A LABEL, IT MUST BE A KNOCKOFF OR IS POORLY MADE.

and

19. ALL LABELS ARE IMPORTANT.

WHEN YOU GET MORE INTO VINTAGE, you will find that some of the very best items are without labels. Labels are great to see, and sometimes help you understand the history of the item, but not all are distinguished. On the flip side, some people removed great labels, perhaps as souvenirs. I once had a 1950s Dior suit without a label, and only by consulting a number of experts was I able to confirm that the Dior jacquard lining wasn't lying!

For some, home-sewn items could be even more interesting. As vintage-lover Corinna said "I feel intensely sentimental about honoring the hours poured into homemade dresses. Plus I suspect that the skill of a seasoned dressmaker in a couture house still couldn't hold a candle to the laser-like focus and hopefulness that would go into a homemade dress sewn during the Great Depression or WWII."

20. IF A GARMENT HAS A NAME ON ITS LABEL, IT'S THE NAME OF A DESIGNER.

OFTEN THERE is a designer name or two behind a label, but the label itself may not give you a clue. One case in point is Suzy Perette—there was no Suzy. See the Vintage Fashion Guild's online *Label Resource* for the story behind the labels.

21. DON'T WORRY ABOUT THE STAINS; YOU CAN JUST DYE IT.

IF YOU ARE a dyeing expert, maybe. Then you will know that some fabrics (assuming they are washable) take dye much better than others, and some older fabrics simply can't stand up to the conditions of a dye bath. I would not suggest purchasing something on the assumption that such a project will work out.

You *can* try to tackle the stains, see page 101.

22: "I LOVE THAT DRESS, BUT I WOULD HAVE NO PLACE TO WEAR IT."

I HEAR THAT myth often, and to this I say, *If you want to get dressed up, get dressed up!*

See the section "You do *so* have somewhere to wear it" on page 126.

1950s SUZY PERETTE DRESS SOLD BY CARLAANDCARLA

How to wear vintage

To GET THE MOST JOY (and the most use!) from your vintage, it helps to understand details of fit, quality, condition, care, and value. But before we tackle these big subjects, let's have a little fun with the subject of how to wear vintage. You aren't alone if you have been tentative about wearing vintage, not knowing how to incorporate it into your wardrobe. Should you wear head-to-toe 1960s mod? Or do you pair a 1970s sweater with modern clothes?

This is really up to you, and both can look great. I often see dos and don'ts columns where the head-to-toe approach is treated as a big mistake. All I can say is if you want to dress like Audrey Hepburn in *Breakfast at Tiffany's* from top to bottom, you have my respect and admiration. Do what makes you look and feel good.

PHOTO EVERETT COLLECTION

The other basic approach of combining eras does appear to be favored, based on a survey of vintage wearers that I recently conducted: 73% responded that they mainly wear a piece or two of vintage mixed in with more modern clothing, 18% wear head-to-toe vintage of mixed eras, and 9% said that, as much as possible, they wear head-to-toe vintage from a single era at one time.

Of the survey respondents, 62% like dresses the best, with strong showings for jewelry, coats, bags, and sweaters. I love dresses most of all too, but if you like vintage jeans, kimonos, or 1950s novelty print skirts best (as did three respondents), great! Vintage really frees you to create looks all your own, with your favorite components. A vintage brooch may be where you start your vintage journey, and if it's the only thing you ever wear that's more than twenty-five years of age, fine!

WHAT'S YOUR DECADE?

I BELIEVE in wearing what you feel good in, but you may feel better (and look better) in some vintage styles more than others. It can be good to cultivate a sense of what flatters you.

Because "vintage clothing" includes any garment twenty years old or older, you have a pretty big range to choose from!

Do you know what your best features are? Consider not just your physique, but your face, your hair, your neck, your ankles, your shoulders—heck, even your knees. There is an era's style that is going to show off your best. In a general sense, the 1920s and '60s fashions favored a straighter, thinner, younger shape, while the late 1940s through the early '60s was the hourglass era. In the 1930s, fashions skimmed slender hips but often had some give with bias-cut fabrics. I consider 1939–46 a somewhat more natural (neither straight nor exaggeratedly curvy) era, as with most of the 1970s. The '80s saw something of a '50s-fit comeback.

Take a look at some styles from the 1910s through the '80s:

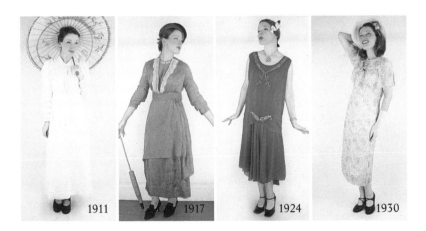

1911   1917   1924   1930

1933   1934   1935   1936

1938   1939   1940   1941

1943   1944   1945   1946

1948   1949   1951   1953

1956   1958   1960   1961

1962   1965   1966   1967

PHOTOS DENISEBRAIN

There are many more silhouettes from these eras; this is just a very general sense. A great online reference is the Vintage Fashion Guild's *Fashion Timeline*. Look for styles or components of styles that will help show you at your best. Many people tell me that they love such-and-such an era and that's all that interests them. If this is your case, you may limit yourself somewhat. I recommend staying open-minded.

One caveat: Before you get too excited about the possibility of regularly wearing *very* vintage (such as 1920s and '30s) and antique clothing, let me caution you: Rare and delicate items need to be treated with respect and care, and may not actually stand up to wearable use. A great example of this, particularly because popular culture is routinely mad for it: 1920s beaded silk dresses. These gorgeous creations are everything good except durable. The weight of the beading, sequins, and/or metallic threads combined with fine silk has just not stood the test of time in many cases. If you find such a dress in wearable condition, you should seriously consider (and I know this hurts) *not* wearing it, or just wearing it briefly for a photo. In the end, clothing is ephemeral, and some items are more so than others.

WHAT'S YOUR VINTAGE-WEARING PERSONA?

As VINTAGE FASHION has become more and more popular, certain vintage-wearing modes have cropped up, each with its own stylish adherents.

Meet the *vintage-wearing personas*, modes of dress you might be inspired to choose every day, or flit between. As I said before, the majority of vintage wearers tend to favor mixing vintage in some form, and mixers of all sorts are included among these types.

Wear-with-All

Not driven by vintage, just looking for a unique, quality vintage piece here and there

Do you want to wear vintage but not broadcast the fact? You may be a Wear-with-All type. Your natural style may be bold or reserved, elegant, flamboyant, or grungy—wearing vintage is not your driving motivator.

For the Wear-with-All persona, you might want to find vintage replacements for modern components of your wardrobe as they wear out. You might find something that is in style right now, only in the better-quality, better-priced, and unique vintage original version. Start with just one piece mixed in with modern clothes and accessories from your closet.

What's easy about this style persona is that you almost can't seem costume-y. You can blend into your work setting, take the dog for a walk, go to a party—and feel attractive but not conspicuously "vintage." You are more likely to hear "I love that!" than "is that vintage?"

The hard part may be coming up with the vintage items that work well for you and your present wardrobe, in the right size—but that's why I've written this book! Really, the hardest part may be showing restraint once you get going with vintage.

WEAR-WITH-ALL HEROINES
Michelle Obama, Amal Clooney

WEAR-WITH-ALL QUOTE
It's not about the dress you wear, but the life you lead in the dress.

—DIANA VREELAND

MICHELLE OBAMA (WHITE HOUSE PHOTO CHUCK KENNEDY)

Time Traveler

The total look, hat-to-shoes right out of a vintage Vogue

This is the easiest and hardest vintage fashion personality, rolled into one. The simple part is that you don't have to figure out if a style works, you just need to recreate a look that you admire. You can choose your outfit and styling literally from a vintage magazine editorial, advertisement, or a movie—you are the costumer and actor in your own period drama.

What's trickier may be finding and putting together the details of the look you want, and then carrying off the look with aplomb. Your look could be seen as costume-y, and you will need to be ready to answer questions about the style and why you are "so dressed up."

Some women pull off this look daily, even in a workplace environment, others dress from hat to shoes in a period look for a special event. This is a persona you might take on here and there—or all the time.

TIME TRAVELER HEROINES
Dita von Teese, Paloma Faith

TIME TRAVELER QUOTE
She's a three page love letter in a world of relationship status updates.

—J. M. STORM

DITA VON TEESE (DPA PICTURE ALLIANCE ARCHIVE/ALAMY)

Walking Work of Art

Creative and bold, using vintage but not necessarily all vintage

This persona is natural for the rare human being, the type of person who might see her body as a canvas for sartorial creativity. Dressing with vintage will give this type the most generous possible palette for self-expression.

Maybe this is the look you really admire but it seems difficult to you. First you have to decide what works, then you have to let go of your inhibitions. The one commonality I see between the protagonists of this style is that they have a signature touch—unusual glasses, giant bracelets, a turban—whatever seems to most suit their style. I believe this style takes a sense of humor. After all, a bit of a smile never hurts when you're being noticed by everyone.

WALKING WORK OF ART HEROINES
Iris Apfel, Anna Piaggi

WALKING WORK OF ART QUOTE
Fashion should be a form of escapism, not a form of imprisonment.
—ALEXANDER MCQUEEN

IRIS APFEL (AF ARCHIVE/ALAMY)

Vintage Mixer

Some, mostly, or all vintage, put together from various eras

Do you want your wardrobe to be mainly vintage yet not feel like you are time traveling from another era? Vintage mixing is the art of putting together an outfit from various vintage components that may date from different decades. You might put a 1950s blouse with 1970s high-waisted jeans, or a 1960s dress with a 1940s bag. What might bring the decades together is some sort of harmony, in color, print, fabric or style.

VINTAGE MIXER HEROINES
Tavi Gevinson, Zooey Deschanel

VINTAGE MIXER QUOTE

Fashion has always been a repetition of ideas, but what makes it new is the way you put it together. —CAROLINA HERRERA

TAVI GEVINSON (DANIEL ZUCHNIK/GETTY IMAGES)

A lot of vintage wearers are wonderful at mixing, but how they choose to mix varies from person to person as well as from day to day. Some Vintage Mixers can relate to Time Travelers, some to Wear-with-Alls, still others border on Walking Works of Art.

Try these subcategories of Vintage Mixer on for size:

Era-Mashing Mixer

The Era-Mashing Mixer is a purist about wearing mostly vintage, but as to which era, they are an iconoclast. For one outfit they may mix a 1940s jacket and hat with a 1970s jumpsuit and 1960s shoes. This might be done with purposeful harmonizing, or ironic wit.

ZEEZSA—HER PERSONAL HASHTAG IS #JUSTBLOODYWEARIT

Specialist Mixer

The Specialist Mixer might be seen as a collector, connoisseur, and wearer of certain favorite vintage items in particular. They may tote vintage handbags, or cuff themselves in vintage Bakelite bracelets, wear vintage modernist-print Vera scarves or pieces from the 1970s by Yves Saint Laurent. Their wearable collections may be estimable.

SANDI FROM LORREL MAE'S VINTAGE COLLECTS AND WEARS BAKELITE BRACELETS

Modern/Vintage Mixer

Modern/Vintage Mixer types may seek out vintage that interprets new styles, or new styles that echo vintage. Not one to set aside the present state of fashion, but also fascinated by the past, the Modern/Vintage Mixer is a creative blender of the old and new.

People that I know in this group are sometimes motivated by the green side of vintage, being anti-fast fashion, careful to be sure their modern fashion purchases are ethically and sustainably made as often as possible. Sometimes their contemporary pieces consist of the basics, and they use vintage as the mainstay of their wardrobes.

NICOLE OF THE BLOG *THE ARTYOLOGIST*

Inspired-by-Vintage Mixer

This mixer contingency may not be able to find what they need in good shape and in the right size (at the right time), or may simply want to wear something that looks vintage that they needn't worry about if jitter-bugging or pruning the rosebush. Often these mixers are close to Time Travelers, their full-on vintage look created with a certain amount of repro vintage-style clothing. The Inspired-by-Vintage Mixer might, for instance, wear repro shoes and jeans with an authentic vintage sweater and scarf.

HARLOW DARLING WEARING A REPRODUCTION VINTAGE DRESS AND SCARF

More mixing tips

Obviously there are many ways to mix vintage into your wardrobe, depending upon your personal preferences. This takes some thought, experimentation, taste, and knowledge, all of which can be honed. Here are some how-to tips that might spur your imagination and focus your style.

Where to start:

- A favorite vintage item—one you have, or one you are considering. Coordinate your choices to highlight this piece.

- A favorite color or fabric.

- A theme, person, or fictional character that you like (e.g., autumn, Josephine Baker, Jean Seberg in *Breathless*).

What to mix:

- Eras (a 1940s red dress with a 1970s red macrame handbag)

- Colors (a blue 1960s shift dress and a '60s sweater in the complementary shade of orange)

- Patterns (a plaid with a ditsy floral in coordinating colors)

- High and low fashion (a 1950s letterman jacket with a gold lamé accordion-pleated skirt)

When you mix vintage pieces up, consider *matching* certain elements:
- Color across eras (a '60s shift with a '90s bolero, both in raspberry pink)

- Fabric prints or textures that relate to one another (velvets from several eras)

- All one era but in an unexpected way (a '70s plaid skirt with an embroidered Mexican blouse from the same time period)

- Timeless elements (a classic white button-down shirt, well-cut trousers, a camel hair wrap coat—doesn't matter the era, these will always be classics)

Do you pin? Try pinning ideas on a Pinterest board or physically pinning images on a bulletin board, or into a scrapbook. Sometimes you don't know what you like until you cluster a number of images together. Sometimes the images will beget new ideas of what your style is becoming. Sometimes when you don't know what the heck to wear that day you can take one look at your board and get a great idea.

Keep doing this, perhaps each season or at least twice a year, because style is not something that should be completely immutable and without reaction to what's going on in your life and the world. Look for images of people wearing vintage in a way that really works for you. Don't copy, just get the gist.

An interesting perspective on vintage mixing was expressed in an Instagram comment from Isabelle, a vintage-loving nurse living in Nice, France: "Clothes have their proper life when you have a few, and they call for each other without you doing anything—The best vintage wearing helpers are the beautiful vintage clothes themselves!"

VINTAGE MIXERS:

1 KHRYSTYNA MARRIOTT / RUBYROBINBOUTIQUE.COM

2 BECKY RUSSELL

3 SUZANNECARILLO.COM / VINTAGE BY SUZANNE

4 LAURA CARTER OF DESERT BELLE VINTAGE

5 @TUNABAKE ON INSTAGRAM

The vintage mindset

QUALITY AND TRUE VALUE

HAVE YOU EVER SEEN the prices in old catalogues and bemoaned the fact that you can't get fashions so inexpensively these days? The truth is, our clothes now are dirt cheap by comparison. I lament the true cost of choosing quantity over quality.

One example: The median U.S. household income is $64,430 as of this writing. According to census records, the median household income in 1940 was $1,368. A coat costing $6.98 in 1940? That would be .51% of a household's income that year. In today's prices (using the Consumer Price Index Inflation Calculator), the coat price would be $128, a mere .19% of our average household income now.

That coat was a real investment in its day.

1939

When you buy a vintage piece, you pay for something that is usually of better quality than the new clothing you are paying for today. As a vintage clothing dealer, I can vouch for the superior quality of most vintage items I come across. In fact, I find it hard to buy modern items in large part because of their lack of quality. Vintage spoils you!

Finer fabrics, linings, better-grade components such as buttons and trims, details like hand-sewn elements and carefully pieced fabric prints—all of these add to the quality of a piece. Those are the reasons why vintage fashion can be wildly economical for its quality.

A word on "newer" vintage quality. A gradual change from better to lesser quality has taken place from the late 1960s through today. Many labels, designers, and makers have transcended this over the decades, but the trend has been toward steadily more disposable, briefly fashionable styles. Right now there are some healthy prices being paid by vintage customers for lesser-made items from the 1970s, '80s, and '90s. The more you know about clothing details and manufacture, the more accurately you will be able to assess the actual value of a vintage clothing item. I don't mean to say that newer vintage items are not worth anything (especially if they make your heart sing), but it is best to arm yourself with the knowledge of their true value. If you want to pay a top price, at least you'll know what you're doing!

In the 1950s, most of what was available to wear in the U.S. was made in the U.S., from the raw materials to the textile, design, and finished product. Union tags on items let you know that fairly paid garment workers made the items.

THE ILGWU, ONCE ONE OF LARGEST LABOR UNIONS IN THE UNITED STATES, WAS ONE OF THE FIRST U.S. UNIONS TO HAVE PRIMARILY FEMALE MEMBERSHIP. (COURTESY OF CMRJB, WORKERS UNITED)

By comparison, Green America's Retailer Scorecard gives Walmart an F, J. C. Penney a D–, and Target a D+ for their use of sweatshops and forced child labor. In choosing a vintage article, you not only recycle it for current use, but you can be fairly confident that it was made by adults who earned a fair wage.

Elizabeth L. Cline's *Overdressed: The Shockingly High Cost of Cheap Fashion* should give even the most inveterate Topshop or Zara shopper pause. She writes: "No one expects to take an H&M shirt to the grave. At prices that often circle around $20, we know the product is not *good quality*. Instead, the quality is *good enough*." The fast fashion model demands cheap labor to create tremendous amounts of clothing that is only briefly fashionable or usable. The economics of this model demand exactly this relationship for the companies that produce the clothes to profit.

Of course this leads to an awful lot of waste. Water, fossil fuels, and energy go into making clothing. Then, as Cline reports, 13 million tons of textile waste is generated annually in the U.S. Of that, only 15% is donated. And of what's being donated, only 20% gets resold.

ALLISON RINALDI WORE THIS DRESS FOR HER WEDDING IN 2011, HER GRANDMOTHER
WORE IT IN 1941. THE DRESS WAS BOUGHT FOR ALLISON'S GREAT-GREAT-GRANDMOTHER'S
WEDDING IN 1884—TALK ABOUT LONGEVITY! (PHOTO JON KOCH)

Vintage clothing is, by contrast, at the top of the charts in "slow fashion," a term that borrows its name from the farm-to-table slow food movement. Fashion, being by its very nature trend-driven and ever-changing, makes it an unlikely candidate for slowing down, but it is a concept that has taken hold. Slow fashion doesn't mean being unfashionable, but it does mean very consciously choosing better and fewer items, fashions that are ethically and environmentally better for the world, and then taking care of them.

Best-in-Slow
Fashion

Vintage and secondhand clothing: Nothing newly made, nothing newly thrown away; plenty of quality and style to go around

Handmade or repurposed by you: The satisfaction of DIY and having just what you want

Newly created by an independent maker or small company: Supporting small businesses and craftspeople

Newly made by a medium to large company that is committed to sustainably and ethically made goods

FROM TOP: COURTESY XTABAY VINTAGE, DESMOND GATIMU/PEXELS,
ARTEM BELIAIKIN/UNSPLASH, THIERRY FILLIEUL/PEXELS

In a comment on one of my blog posts, reader Louise shared what she appreciates most about vintage clothing: "You are not supporting sweatshops. No new materials are being consumed. And most vintage clothing sellers are small businesses—you are supporting an individual rather than a multinational corporation." For her, the greatest value in vintage clothing is in its impact on the world, economically and environmentally. I have talked with others who are most attentive to the fine construction of the vintage they collect.

No matter which reason fits you best, vintage is valuable.

You may notice that in this book I don't write that a 1950s dress should cost *X*. I don't think there will ever be a point at which one would be able to say that a certain vintage piece *should* cost a certain amount. Dealers set prices that are based on the availability of each item and the work the seller may have to do to get the item ready for use. The quality, condition, scarcity, and desirability of a piece influences the going rate. Some dealers also have a certain right to say that with their knowledge and experience they can offer items of a certain caliber for a certain amount. With all these variables, there is no magic formula for pricing vintage.

Looking through thrift stores or even in vintage shops online, you may be fortunate to find some great vintage items that are really inexpensive, and if so, more power to you. The hunt can be a thrill, although you may not find what you are looking for. I have a friend in a big city who says that in looking in secondhand shops and garage and estate sales, she hasn't seen any vintage dating from before the 1970s for some time. The 1940s and '50s fashions that I love so dearly aren't to be found in some areas. If you are interested in 1920s and '30s styles, the pickings are slim no matter where you are. Rarity does indeed increase value.

Condition is also a large part of the value. A great vintage item in very flawed condition is possibly worth less than a relatively lower-quality item in excellent condition. The more you know about what constitutes a great item (such as fine materials, a valued designer, rarity) and great condition, the more you will be able to assess this.

Value may also be judged in terms of how long a garment has been around, and how long it might continue to be around. Taking care of your vintage clothing (whether through cleaning or mending) will certainly contribute to its long-term value since it will get much more use if its condition and wearability are maintained.

And a great vintage seller—the kind that is knowledgeable, passionate, resourceful, careful, honest, and dependable—is a bit rare too. If you find you like and trust certain sellers, you may wish to visit them more than once. As Louise wrote, these are small business owners who will appreciate your support.

CARING FOR VINTAGE: A WORTHY COMMITMENT

WHEN YOUR CAT AND YOU had a fabric-ripping tussle, an insect ate your best sweater for lunch, or you stepped through the hem of your best gown, it's hard to imagine how a vintage favorite will ever be wearable again, but don't despair, many flaws can be discreetly fixed or camouflaged by a skilled seamstress, if not you. Refusing to give up on a great garment is a very vintage virtue. You've heard the expression "make do and mend"? It dates from WWII, when rationing and shortages were par for the course, but today, with an awareness of the impact mass consumption has on the planet, doesn't making do and mending seem modern?

If you have taken the time to find a great vintage item, and it looks and feels wonderful on you, then you know it is worth taking the time and effort to clean and mend as needed. While vintage clothing may have age-related wear and tear, it was often better made (and out of better materials) than modern clothing. It was made to be cleaned and fixed.

Our parents, grandparents, and great-grandparents did not live with disposable items the way we do now, clothing included. Purchases were made carefully, alterations were done, care was taken, mends were made, and quite a bit of wear was expected over years of use. If you find a vintage clothing item you love, consider grabbing the baton and wearing the item with the same care and thought that was used thirty, sixty, even ninety years ago. If you do, you may pass the item on for further use in thirty years!

If you are accustomed to tossing your clothes in the washer and dryer, never ironing or mending, care of your vintage may take a little getting used to. I'm the laziest person alive, yet I have learned some systems for not only taking care of my vintage clothing, but even enjoying the process. Some favorite activities are ironing a cotton button-down shirt (while sipping a glass of wine!), hanging wash out on the laundry line to dry (because I love the smell of the clothes when I bring them in!), and finding and sewing on vintage buttons when they are missing.

Trust me, it is a very good feeling when you get to see your beautiful vintage pieces looking clean, polished, in excellent repair, and ready to go!

Why should YOU wear vintage clothing?

1. It looks fabulous! Vintage clothing is often designed with much more detail than modern clothing, even on the simplest day dress. The fabrics are at the very least different, and at the very most stunningly rich and beautiful. Oh, and the colors!...Try a '30s peach, a '40s navy, a '50s combination of blues, purples and olive or a '60s hot pink and riotous orange. Even greys and blacks are different. Then there's the construction, from elaborate darting to finely sewn buttonholes, so often no detail is spared. Whether the fashions were sewn by decently-paid American factory workers or home seamstresses, there is such great quality in vintage! **2. It is recycling!** Why go and buy another new thing (and have you noticed how much new stuff is vintage inspired or washed and treated to look very worn?). Why not just have the real thing, save the raw materials, waste, and energy. And that includes your own! Used is so, so good. So many things are better when worn: Shoes are broken in just enough, leather jackets have character, prairie dresses look like they've seen the prairie... **3. It has karma!** Sometimes it is a wedding announcement in a coat pocket, other times it is just a feeling you have that somehow this dress, this pair of shoes, has been around a dance floor with the handsomest man in Cuba, ca.1947! It is like wearing history, and sharing someone else's story. So many sweet kisses, sunny days gone by, theater openings, and jobs well done are imbedded in vintage clothes. **4. It might fit you better!** New clothes are cut according to standards that are dictated by the garment industry and fashion sensibilities. But what if you are cut more like Marilyn Monroe than the current trend? Or what if you are as gamine as Audrey Hepburn? There is a time in fashion for you! Look at the measurements on the clothing, they never coincide exactly with modern sizing, and you are likely to find a decade, a cut, and an article of dress that is so YOU darling that it seems like the designer had only you in mind. **5. It is generally a very good bargain!** So often vintage clothing, even in the priciest high-falutin' vintage boutique, is much less expensive than new clothing. If you are looking for brand names, designers, or just good-looking clothing, you will definitely find it for less, and almost always of a better quality, than new clothing ever can be. **6. It is not what everyone else has!** The cool thing is, even if you and all your friends wear vintage, you will all be dressed in unique and totally gorgeous ways. And you will never, I repeat NEVER, run into someone wearing exactly the same clothes. You know you are special, so why dress like someone else? **7. It will remind you of interesting times gone by!** Is it reliving your childhood in penny loafers? Taking a swirl in a swing dress like your mom once wore? Cruising the streets in a local bowling league shirt? Not only is this karma (see #3 above), it is connection to very special people, places and history that you know, love and want. You are living history, not just covering yourself to evade indecency laws! **8. It lets you play new roles! In a different mood?** Want to be someone just a little different today? How about a Mod, a 1930s femme fatale, a suffragette, a USO starlet, a flapper, a New Look untouchable beauty, a hippie, a war bond rationer, a dust bowl prairie girl, a First Lady, a princess, a siren, a punk? Why limit yourself to mere reality and the here and now? **9. Vintage highlights your uniqueness!** Want to go up a notch in the fascination quotient? You will be unique (ain't no one dressing just like you), beautiful (because you have found the just right style of all time for you), sensitive (you're saving the environment after all) and intelligent (look at all the money you have saved).

Great first vintage items: Accessible accessories

By now you probably have some ideas about different ways you might wear vintage and you're all on board with the vintage mindset. You want to wear vintage and look great in it. How do you get started?

I recommend starting with an accessory. Why? Accessories are afford-able, stylistically flexible, and one-size-fits-all. Well, most of the time—it's true that a signed Miriam Haskell brooch can go for hundreds of dollars, not every purse or pair of earrings will go with every outfit, and items such as hats or gloves do present some fit considerations. But in general, vintage accessories are great gateway pieces for beginners and can be easily in-corporated into most modern wardrobes.

Brooches

One of my absolute favorite recommendations is a vintage brooch, because their character and quality can set the tone for an outfit and spur sartorial creativity. Go spare and refined or go over-the-top gaudy. Choose Deco rhinestones, earthy wood, or funky plastic; your initials or your favorite breed of dog. Try searching "vintage brooch" on Etsy and see what you are drawn to.

PHOTOS DENISEBRAIN

35

Brooches have traditionally been worn somewhere near the neckline. There's nothing wrong with that, but consider using one on a clip in your hair, in a scatter of pins across your shoulder, or on your pants cuff or a fabric handbag. Vintage brooches make a fascinating focal point clustered by theme—and they give people a great reason to strike up a conversation!

In a comment on one of my blog posts, reader Pam shared her suggestion for getting started with vintage: "...if there's a piece a loved one has (or had) with some sort of sentimental value, wearing that piece might be a great, heart-centered way to begin. It's a tangible way to time travel that has personal meaning."

That is such a great point, and so often there is a brooch, necklace, or other item still in the family from times gone by. You can wear your mother's vintage brooch exactly the way she did—or with your own twist.

ANGELA NEUSTATTER WROTE ABOUT KEEPING THE MEMORY OF HER MOTHER ALIVE
BY WEARING HER CLOTHES AND ACCESSORIES, INCLUDING THIS BROOCH.
(*DAILY MAIL ONLINE*, ARTICLE 2051149, OCTOBER 2011)

Handbags

Another good choice for a starting piece is a vintage bag. In general, vintage bags are not as large as the everything-but-the-kitchen-sink types we often carry now. But while a large vintage tote may not be easy to find, there are lots of wonderful choices in medium to small bags and especially evening bags.

Don't be surprised if you eventually find yourself collecting certain types or makes of vintage bags—they are addictive!

Scarves

Of course, other items without fit issues are great starters too. Love scarves? Then hooray, because there are so many gorgeous vintage scarves to be found.

And there are as many vintage-wearing style inspirations as there are beautiful vintage scarves!

I'm sure you can think of other vintage items without fit concerns. (Do I hear umbrellas? Earrings?) These also make good first steps into the land of vintage.

B&W PHOTOS EVERETT COLLECTION, COLOR PHOTOS DENISEBRAIN

VINTAGE SCARVES SOLD BY NORTHSTAR VINTAGE

Some more favorite vintage accessories

HERE ARE MORE vintage accessories, each with some fit issues to consider. In every case (glasses, hats, shoes and gloves) you will find variety, quality, value, and style by going vintage.

SEE YOURSELF IN VINTAGE GLASSES

A FAVORITE FOR ADDING GREAT FLAIR to a modern wardrobe is a pair of vintage sunglasses, or if you are ready to go further, regular glasses. I love my 1950s and '60s plastic frames with new prescription lenses. Two of my frames were deadstock and in flawless shape, but one had to be adjusted a couple of times by my optician because the plastic wanted to travel back to its original contour after all the years it had been cooped up in its case. The plastic held up well under pressure, and eventually relented to fit me perfectly. I've even updated the lenses.

Look how fabulous these '50s frames look on vintage-wearing Mary:

COURTESY OF MARY BILLS

Casey (another vintage fan) told me, "I don't know if I could go back to normal glasses...[Vintage glasses] are a great startup item. I had lots of occasion items, but the glasses were the first step into daily wear."

Glasses are not without fit issues, so it is important to get some measurements.

If you have modern frames that fit you well, check the frame's size; it will most likely be found inside the temple, occasionally on the inside of the bridge. The numbers you see will be the eye size, the bridge size, and the temple size, each shown in millimeters. Eye size isn't *your* eye size, but the width of each lens; 40–62 is the usual range. The bridge size is the distance between the lenses at their closest point. That size ought to be between 14 and 24. The temple (in the 120–150 range) is the length from the front of the frame to the end of the earpiece.

Vintage frames most likely will not have a size in them, and your modern frames' size numbers may have worn away. Do not despair! You can find the right width to fit you using a stiff ruler that measures millimeters. Measure your face from temple to temple just below your eyes. Try to stay close (like within several millimeters) to this width for a vintage frame that will fit you well. Vintage sellers online need to provide measurements for the frames they offer—ask if you don't see what you need to make an informed choice.

If you require bifocal or progressive lenses, you may need to check the lens height of the vintage frames you are considering. Although these lenses can fit into most frames, if the frames you are looking at have a small vertical size you should check with your optometrist to see if the frames will work with your prescription.

Sunglasses may certainly be larger, depending on the style.

So many styles of vintage frames are influencing modern styles—Wayfarer, aviator, round, cat eye. Why not seek out the originals?

LET VINTAGE HATS GO TO YOUR HEAD

I'LL SAY IT RIGHT NOW: I have a big head. I didn't think I could wear hats because I had the experience of modern one-size-fits-all styles not fitting. Then I discovered that there are styles galore of vintage hats that have a fit that works for many, including me. My personal favorites are from the first half of the 1940s, when all the pent-up whimsy and fashionability that couldn't be budgeted and rationed into clothing choices during WWII could go to a girl's head.

PHOTO DENISEBRAIN

For those of you who think sure, that's fine for *you*, but *I* can't wear a hat, let alone a *vintage* hat, let me tell you a true story: A friend of mine (not a vintage wearer) found a vintage hat that she loved. It wasn't over-the-top, just a nice, simple navy blue felt hat with a medium brim, dating from the mid-to-late 1940s. My friend took a bus to work daily, and her commute involved crossing a busy street to get to the bus stop. The day she started wearing her vintage hat, cars stopped for her to cross, people commented on how good she looked—and she *felt* good! Don't underestimate your ability to wear a vintage hat and make it your own.

POLLY BERGEN IN 1951 WEARING A HAT NOT UNLIKE MY FRIEND'S
(MONDADORI/EVERETT COLLECTION)

If you still feel awkward and afraid you aren't right for hats, consider that the *hat* might not be right for *you*.

Most every modern woman has, at some point, considered her face shape when choosing how to wear her hair. I'll bet you know whether your face is oval, round, square, diamond, or heart shaped, how your hair interacts with that shape, and what hairstyles are best for you.

Women used to know these same things about hats. I have purchased collections of hats from the estates of women I never set eyes on, but based on their hats I could tell you things about them, maybe even their height, coloring, face shape, and style.

There are some basics to consider when looking at hats.

If you are petite, a small hat will highlight your look without overwhelming you. Cloches, as well as the fitted hat styles of the 1930s, 1940s, and 1950s, may work best. Also consider small pillbox hats from the 1950s and '60s. If you are more statuesque, the opposite can apply. Too small a hat might be lost on you, and you can balance your features with something on a larger scale. There are choices going back to the Edwardian era as well as wide-brim cloches from circa 1930. Look for picture hats and outgoing shapes from the 1940s, '50s, '60s and '70s.

One thing that may make a vintage hat appear lackluster on you is how you wear your hair. I have naturally straight, medium-length hair and find that some pre-1960s hats look best when I add a little lift by way of a French roll, a few curls, a comb pulling one side up, or even just a ponytail. Experiment a little with your hair, perhaps giving a nod to past hairstyles while keeping your own basic look.

The face shape diagram on the next page dates from the 1940s. Look at the way the face shape is enhanced or altered by the hairstyle and the hat.

All that said, there are so many style rules that are better off broken. Do you have wide-set eyes? The conventional wisdom would be to deemphasize the width at that point on your face. But if you love to emphasize this interesting feature, then let a line of your hat be at eye level.

Eyes, in general, will be a strong focus with a hat veil or a tilted brim. Slightly hidden, any feature is more alluring, but especially the eyes. Does asymmetry or symmetry work best on your face? Hats can emphasize or deemphasize. Your whole face is in focus with a hat. Don't be afraid of that fact—your hair is already bringing focus to your face, so a hat gives you even more options for personalizing your style.

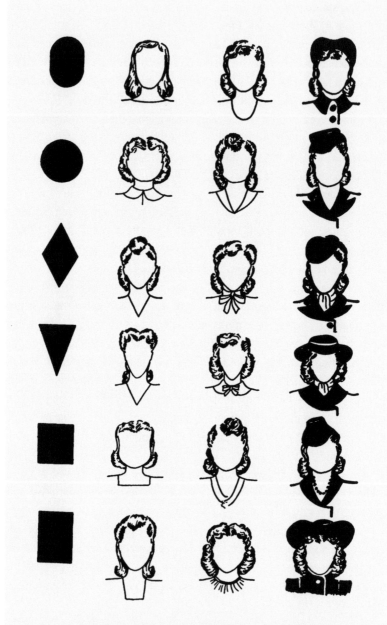

HAIRLINES AND HAT LINES ALTER CONTOURS

FROM *CLOTHES WITH CHARACTER*, BY HAZEL THOMPSON CRAIG
AND OLA DAY RUSH, 1946 ED., HATHITRUST

Consider a hat in a shade to complement your own color, and your wardrobe's.

Shape, size, angle, symmetry, era, hairstyle, color—does this seem like just too much to think about?

The effort is all a matter of perspective. Is it any different from spending time to style your hair every morning or learning how to get your makeup picture-perfect?

What we have going for us right now, hat-wise, is free rein. Many are wearing different eras of clothing and accessories with increasing knowledge and sophistication. Sometimes a vintage hat is part of a single-era costume; other times it adds some playfulness to a modern style. Allow your taste to answer the question, *Does this work*?

It sometimes helps to get impressions from famous faces with varying hats. Which hat do you most like on Ava Gardner? Why? How does her hairstyle interact with the hat?

PHOTOS EVERETT COLLECTION

I know what you're thinking—Ava Gardner is so beautiful she could wear anything and look sensational. But look at some "regular" women— would any of them look better without her hat? I don't think so either.

COLLECTION OF VINTAGE PHOTO BOOTH IMAGES

I AM A GREAT DEVOTEE of vintage shoes. Vintage shoe options can wow you with style and choice.

Do I need to tell you that it is impossible to buy anything like this in a modern shoe?

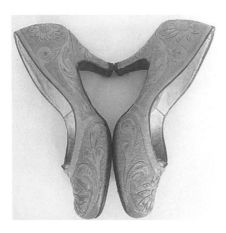

HAND-TOOLED LEATHER PUMPS, 1950s

Vintage shoes are wonderful, but there are caveats. Age takes a greater toll on an item that handles your weight and activity so tangibly, so the condition is critical. However, many vintage shoes are of such excellent quality that when their condition is also excellent, you can expect to get a lot of wear. Although I wouldn't recommend this to a novice vintage wearer, at some point you may be able to spot a pair of vintage shoes whose uppers are in excellent shape and the wear to the soles can be addressed by having the shoes resoled by a shoe repair shop that you have learned to trust. I had that wonderful pair of 1950s hand-tooled leather shoes from Mexico resoled for $45. I am sure they have decades of life left.

Replacing heel caps alone is usually relatively inexpensive, and having a heel cap replaced for something like $4-5 is a very good investment. But when wear goes through the heel cap into the heel, the cost will be four or five times greater. Although I strongly recommend finding shoes in excellent condition if you are a novice vintage shoe buyer, know that later repairs and maintenance will be easier if the shoes are leather instead of man-made material. Unused authentic vintage shoes are available (at this writing, for instance, a Vintage Sole's website sells only unused vintage shoes), and if you find some that suit you, you are likely to get great wear from them.

Larger sizes in vintage shoes are a bit limited because the average woman used to have smaller feet. According to a 2014 article in *The Independent*, the average woman's shoe size in the U.S. of the 1960s was 6 ½, while it was 7 ½ in the 1970s. Now the average woman's shoe size is 8 ½ to 9.

I have a collection of vintage shoes in sizes 9 and 9 ½. My modern U.S. size is 9M, and vintage shoes in this relatively large size are not very common, so I keep many that I find, but you *can* find vintage shoes in size 9 and up, so don't despair even if you wear a size 10 or 11.

Vintage shoe sizes, unlike clothing, are similar to modern shoe sizes, so my size 9M is a vintage size 9M, providing that:

- the shoes were made in the U.S.,

- the maker's sizing wasn't too different from the standard, and

- the toes aren't too pointed or the heels too high.

So I also sometimes wear vintage size 9 ½, depending on the style. When you are coveting a pair of vintage shoes online, you will do well to measure your own shoes in as similar a style as possible, taking into account the width at the ball of the foot and the length from toe to heel, with both measurements taken inside the shoe, flat on the insole. Be as persnickety as possible in measuring because size differences are sometimes a matter of mere sixteenths of an inch. Keep in mind that the length of a pointed toe on a shoe is not entirely usable space.

Some vintage shoes have no size marked, or the size has become unreadable. In that case it is imperative you know the length of the shoe, measured on the insole. These insole length and width measurements should be given for the vintage shoe you covet; if they aren't, ask the seller.

Here's a chart that shows shoe sizes and their lengths. These measurements vary depending on the source, but I chose sizing that seemed most in sync with the shoe lengths and sizes I find.

women's shoe size conversions

US sizes	EURO sizes	UK sizes	inches	cm
4	35	2	8.1875"	20.8
4.5	35	2.5	8.375"	21.3
5	35-36	3	8.5"	21.6
5.5	36	3.5	8.75"	22.2
6	36-37	4	8.875"	22.5
6.5	37	4.5	9.0625"	23
7	37-38	5	9.25"	23.5
7.5	38	5.5	9.375"	23.8
8	38-39	6	9.5"	24.1
8.5	39	6.5	9.6875"	24.6
9	39-40	7	9.875"	25.1
9.5	40	7.5	10"	25.4
10	40-41	8	10.1875"	25.9
10.5	41	8.5	10.3125"	26.2
11	41-42	9	10.5"	26.7
11.5	42	9.5	10.6875"	27.1
12	42-43	10	10.875"	27.6

A lot of vintage shoes are stamped with a size that includes the width, which—*caveat emptor*—is often narrow. Narrow in vintage shoes can be designated as N, S (for "slim"), or A. You can also find widths as narrow as 4A or AAAA ("quads," I have heard some older women call them). One rogue trick I occasionally use with vintage shoes is to wear a longer but narrower size than my usual. If I compare my measurements to those of a shoe marked size 9 ½ or 10 narrow, I will sometimes find a good fit, as the widths get slightly wider with longer sizes. This is also called diagonal sizing, as on a chart you are able to try the sizes diagonally up and down from your own, taking in wider and narrower widths.

US women's shoe size	4	5	6	7	8	9	10
N/AA					X		
A					X		
M/B					**X**		
C				X			
W/D					x		
E							
XW/EE							

Have you seen a size stamped in a vintage shoe with two widths indicated? This means the shoe was made on a combination last. The wider width indicated is for the ball of the foot, while the narrower is the heel width. In a shoe with this type of last, the heel will always be two widths narrower, so a B width will have an AA heel and an A will have an AAA heel. If your heel tends to slip out of your shoes, combination lasts are a godsend, and they are not at all common among modern manufacturers. Online sellers should show a photograph of the size stamp, or describe how the size is designated in a vintage shoe, along with including the length and width.

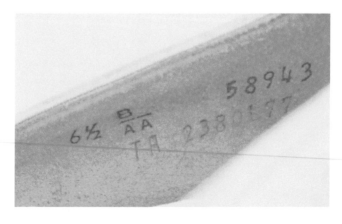

PHOTO DENISEBRAIN

I RECENTLY WENT to an event introducing a vintage fashion collection. A number of people attending were attired to give vintage style a nod, but one woman stood out for her beautiful complete ensemble of excellently fitted 1950s dress suit, hat, shoes, bag, makeup, and hair. Everything seemed in place for a period-perfect ensemble and she was wearing the clothing with panache, but when someone asked why she wasn't wearing gloves she said, "I never know how to wear them—the etiquette, you know?"

If, like her, you love the look of vintage gloves but are afraid you'll get it wrong, keep reading.

Etiquette books with sections covering glove wear wound down by the 1970s. Not that all glove use disappeared then, but with the casualness of the times gloves just didn't play the part they once did. You can still find advice on glove etiquette for brides—and the basics haven't changed substantially since the time when gloves were de rigueur—but now wearing decorative gloves is almost always a matter of taste.

Essentially, the glove-wearing rules from their heyday years of the twentieth century are common sense. See if you can predict which of these are dos and which are don'ts according to Edith Heal's 1961 booklet for the Hansen Glove Corporation, *Gloves: Fashion and Etiquette*.

Do you or don't you?...

1. Eat with gloves on

2. Keep gloves on in a receiving line

3. Wear gloves in a place of worship

4. Play cards with gloves on

5. Apply makeup with gloves on

6. Remove gloves at the dining table

7. Drink with gloves on

8. Wear short gloves to a white tie affair

9. Wear a ring on the outside of your glove (answers next page)

Answers:
1. Don't, 2. Do, 3. Do, 4. Don't, 5. Don't, 6. Do, 7. Don't, 8. Don't, 9. Don't

Even though you probably got these right or see the reason for the correct answer, there are small details which, when you are not privy to glove-wearing rules on a regular basis, could seem foreign.

But first, let's be honest: Not too many people care if you are wearing gloves correctly anymore. The use of gloves is mainly practical now, and the decorative glove is almost completely optional.

And decorative they certainly can be. So long as you are not the one trying for a period-perfect look, you can probably just use your common sense about when the gloves would be better removed than worn. If you wish to employ vintage-style glove etiquette, I can suggest seeking guidelines from your era of choice. After I heard that well-dressed woman say she didn't feel confident in wearing gloves, I went looking for vintage glove advice, and there are plenty of resources. For all things mid-century etiquette, try the 1948 *Vogue's Book of Etiquette* by Millicent Fenwick.

Vintage gloves often have numbered sizes, usually stamped inside. Your modern gloves are probably one-size-fits-all, or perhaps S, M, L, or XL, but vintage gloves were sized more precisely based on the circumference of the hand. To find your glove size, circle your hand with a cloth measuring tape at its widest part, excluding your thumb. The number you get, usually between 6" and 9" (15.2 and 22.9 cm) in half-inch increments, is your glove size. There are variations in sizing with vintage gloves as with all other vintage garments, but gloves aren't the world's most difficult to wear in a slightly off size. Almost all vintage gloves were made of a material with give. A very firmly stretchy and sturdy knit fabric called simplex was often used for vintage gloves in the decades around the middle of the twentieth century. Leather too has give, and nearly always was expected to stretch to "fit like a glove" over time. If a vintage seller does not include the size, you should ask for the circumference of the glove at the middle of the hand.

Glove lengths are sometimes given by name, and sometimes by button length, whether or not there are buttons. A vintage brochure from the Hansen Glove Corporation shows both:

... a certain feeling for fashion
... a certain feeling for fit
... a certain feeling of perfection
when you wear the correct length in a

HANSEN glove

SHOULDER
(20 Button)

BELOW ELBOW
(10 Button)

MID-ARM
(8 Button)

ABOVE ELBOW
(12 Button)

OPERA
(16 Button)

BRACELET
(4 Button)

SHORTIE
(1 Button)

Dolores del Rio wore a sequined gown coordinated with opera-length gloves in this publicity shot for the 1938 movie *International Settlement*:

20TH CENTURY FOX/EVERETT COLLECTION

Figuring out vintage fit and size

OF THE HANDFUL of Really Important Issues when choosing vintage clothing, fit is probably number one for most people. There's quite a lot to cover, so let's get started.

THE IMPORTANCE OF MEASUREMENTS

THERE IS NO STANDARD by which vintage sellers collectively describe sizes, but let's be fair, there is no precise standard for modern clothing either!

Sometimes you'll see a vintage item that has its original tag or label with the size marked on it, but don't confuse this with current sizing. **Vintage sizes do not coincide with modern sizes, nor are they predictable when compared with other items from the same era**. In her study of advertisements in *Vogue* magazine from 1922 to 1999, Alaina Zulli found a great deal of irregularity, with a generally decreasing size number through the decades, due to so-called vanity sizing. As summarized in 2011, Ms. Zulli found that in the Sears catalogue of 1937 for instance, a woman with a 32" bust would have worn a size 14. She would have worn a size 8 by 1967, and today, she's wearing a size 0.[1] Fit is all about measurements, not stated sizes.

I have tried to at least codify my own modern size estimates for the vintage items I have for sale, based on an assortment of websites' and catalogues' size charts. Other vintage sellers have done something similar. However, I would recommend that if you see U.S. size 6, say, or XL, even in **my** listings, *do not assume it is the same as your idea of size 6 or XL*. Go straight for the measurements and compare those to your own.

Many sellers, including me, suggest that you compare the measurements of an item you're interested in with something similar of your own that fits you well. This is great if indeed you have a piece that is similar to the vintage item in key ways, for instance both are made of woven, non-stretchy fabric and are fitted in the same ways. I will later make suggestions about how to choose items even if you have nothing similar.

---

1. Clifford, Stephanie. "One Size Fits Nobody: Seeking a Steady 4 or a 10." *New York Times*, April 24, 2011.

When should you ask for further help from an online vintage seller? By all means ask if there are no/not enough measurements or the condition is not described. A seller who offers almost no information may be a beginner or simply not very skillful. One characteristic that good sellers share is that their listings include most or all of the information you need to make an informed decision. Most good sellers will be happy to guide you if you need further help with the size or some other aspect. Just remember, don't ask if that 1950s dress is a size 6—ask about the item's measurements.

So now that you understand the importance of measurements for fit, here are the most common measurements you will need for clothing:

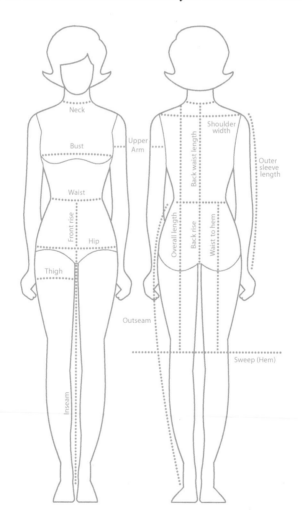

It is an extremely good idea to have someone help you with these measurements, at least the ones that would require advanced contortionism to manage on your own. Use a cloth measuring tape and keep it straight and snug but not tight as you measure. Stand tall and relaxed and don't suck in, especially for the bust and waist measures.

Bust: With your bra on, measure around your body at the fullest part of your bust.

Under-bust measure: Measure around your body just under your bust.

Waist: Measure around the smallest part of your waist, just above your belly button.

Hips: With heels together, measure around the fullest part of your hips, about 8" (20.3 cm) down from your waist.

Shoulder width: Imagine lines going straight up from your armpits to your shoulders in back. Measure from this point on one shoulder to the other, across the back.

Outer sleeve length: Measure from the tip of your shoulder to your wrist along the outside of your arm.

Upper arm: Measure around the fullest part of your upper arm.

Neck: Wrap the tape around your neck about 1" (2.5 cm) above the point where your shoulder meets your neck.

Back waist length: Measure from the base of your neck to your waist in back.

Inseam: While standing straight, measure from the groin to the place where you would like the hem of the pants to fall (ankle or floor).

Outer leg length: Measure from the waist to the point where the hem of the pants will fall.

Rise (front and back): Measure from the groin to your waist at center front for the front rise, and at center back for the back rise.

Allow me to digress a moment here. **You can be any size and look great; you just have to be honest about the size you really are.** For instance, when you measure your waist, *don't suck in or you'll have to live with permanent duck face while wearing too-tight clothes.* If you lose that weight you've been meaning to lose or whittle your waist with exercise, you can find a new vintage frock or alter what you have. But now is now—and you deserve to look and feel great right now! There are vintage foundation garments that will help you modify your size somewhat and we'll touch on that more advanced material later, but for this moment, let's stick with the basics.

Now, what vintage garment are you going to look for first—remembering that we are taking this one step at a time? My suggestion is a sweater because 1) a sweater's fit is flexible—you are practically guaranteed success—and 2) vintage sweaters are the best!

FINDING A VINTAGE SWEATER: THE BENEFIT OF STRETCH

THERE ARE MANY STYLES of sweaters, from chunky knits to fitted Sweater Girl styles, cardigans, short sleeves and sleeveless, beaded, appliquéd, embroidered, hand knit, and major vintage designer labels.

CLOCKWISE, FROM TOP LEFT:

1950s SWEATER JACKET ON APRIL
@LA_VELVET_BELLE ON INSTAGRAM

'80s NOVELTY DESIGN SWEATER FROM
SMALL EARTH VINTAGE

'50s BEADED CARDIGAN FROM
JUMBLELAYA

'60s SEQUINED SWEATER TOP FROM
MORNING GLORIOUS VINTAGE

What do you like in a modern sweater? Something you could wear skiing, a simple basic, or something a bit flashy? If you're looking for warm and thick, try searching for vintage sweaters using keywords like Nordic, Irish (also Irish fisherman, Aran), ski, Fair Isle, Icelandic, boyfriend, chunky, and cable knit. Sweater Girl sweaters are fitted, usually 1950s to '60s in vintage, and often waist length. Look for soft lambswool blends, angora, and cashmere—add beads, sequins, or embroidery to your search for something even dressier.

When it comes to basics, I love vintage cashmere sweaters. They beat most modern cashmere knits in the quality-to-price ratio hands down. Cashmere is light, soft, and warm, and it's not likely to irritate the skin of any but a tiny fraction of the most sensitive wearers. Vintage cashmere knits come in a wide range of styles and colors—they are a practical luxury.

A vintage Scottish-made cashmere sweater like this one from Big Yellow Taxi Vintage is almost guaranteed to lower your heating bill!

COURTESY BIG YELLOW TAXI VINTAGE

The appropriate fit for knits varies with the style. If you like a Sweater Girl fitted style, look for a sweater with a bust measurement about the same as your own. Very often the hem of a sweater is ribbed; ribbing is stretchier than a plain stitch, as well as being sturdier. What that means is that you don't need to worry if the measurement of a ribbed hem is smaller than your own waist or hip measurement, where the hem will fit. One caveat: If the sweater is a cardigan and worn tight at the bust, it may gap along the buttoned placket.

If what you are after is a thick, chunky knit, you may want it to be larger than your own measurement at the bust. I would allow at least 1–2" (2.5–5 cm) of ease (we'll discuss "ease" in more detail soon).

Look carefully at the condition of vintage sweaters. Holes can be mended, but when you're just starting out with vintage, look for a sweater that's in excellent shape, clean, and either hole-free or with just one or two tiny mended holes in inconspicuous places.

Now that you've taken a look at sweater knits, you are ready to delve into woven apparel. Fit is so important in choosing clothing items without much or any stretch.

FINDING A VINTAGE SWING COAT: FOCUSING ON THE KEY MEASUREMENT

A GREAT VINTAGE ITEM for beginners (and experts too!) is a flaring coat or jacket. These chic, perpetually stylish items can date from practically any time in the twentieth century and work for a range of sizes, even for maternity sometimes. With all vintage clothing you need to focus on the measurement that is the most fitted, and for a swing coat, that measurement is usually the shoulder width. Think of this style as just one step more fitted than a cape, which also makes a great vintage choice. Search for the terms "swing coat" and "tent coat" as well as "flaring."

LEFT TO RIGHT: CHIC, EASY-FIT COATS COURTESY OF KRYSTLE DESANTOS; RUBY THREADS VINTAGE; ROAD LESS TRAVELLED 2; AND POSIES FOR LULU VINTAGE (POSIESFORLULUVINTAGE.COM)

Now that you have some knowledge of your measurements and sizing, are you eager to find that perfect Joan Holloway-in-*Mad Men* dress? I'm eager to help you!

A 1950s to early '60s sheath dress like the character Joan Holloway often wore on the popular show *Mad Men* is almost always designed to highlight an hourglass shape, with a relatively fitted waist and a waist seam that doesn't usually have any stretch. Just as the fit focus for swing coats was the shoulders, here the fit focus is most often on the waist measurement.

1960s SARONG-STYLE
SHEATH DRESS BY
TORI RICHARD HONOLULU,
SOLD BY KITTY GIRL
VINTAGE

You now know your waist measure; what you also need in order to be able to enjoy yourself in your vintage dress is a little extra space. This is called "wearing ease."

How much ease do you need? Each of us is a little different in our fit preferences, but we all need to breathe, and most everyone needs to sit, walk, and move her arms. The minimum ease needed for wearing comfort in a fitted dress made of woven fabric is:

1 ½–2 ½" (3.8–6.4 cm) at the bust

¾–1" (2–2.5 cm) at the waist

2–3" (5–7.5 cm) at the hip

So, let's say you have a 28" (71.1 cm) waist, you will want to look for a vintage dress that measures about 29" (73.7 cm) at its waist.

Generally, for clothing made of a non-stretchy woven fabric, someone on the smaller end of sizes can comfortably go with the least wearing ease, while someone on the larger side will want to go with the higher ease measurements for comfort and a visually pleasing fit. By contrast, a garment made of a knit fabric can have no ease or even negative ease (in the case of a swimsuit, for instance) for a proper fit.

Another kind of ease is "design ease," which is part of the cut of the clothing. Every era has a variety of styles and fits, and the ease will vary with the cut of the garment. If you are looking to fit a 1960s flaring tent dress made of a woven fabric, the design ease at the bust will be close to the wearing ease, but the design ease at the waist and hip will be much greater. For a strapless 1950s formal, there may be very little design ease through the bodice because the dress might not stay up if it isn't properly tight! I think we can put up with very little wearing ease for more formal—and briefer!—occasions.

Even if you prefer a tighter fit in most of your modern clothing, please consider the age of the vintage garment and its fabric when choosing what ease you need. A vintage garment made of delicate or loosely woven fabric can show pulling along its vertical seams or even rip if worn too tightly. Thankfully, because of its construction, that 1950s strapless gown is more likely to be tolerant of a close fit. A 1920s beaded silk chiffon dress, on the other hand, is not going to tolerate any tightness.

Looking online, you may spot the waist measure you want for a vintage sheath dress, but the bust and hip measures look too big. That is not uncommon when comparing 1950s to modern sizing. The female body has gone through many fashion ideals, with fits that accentuate and exaggerate those ideals.

No matter what era of clothing you fancy, you have to choose by the measurement that most challenges the wearing ease you need, So, if you're looking at a 1960s shift dress that has plenty of ease for your waist but is a bit too slim in the bust and hip, you will want to look until you find another shift with the ease you need at the bust and hip. Likewise, if you see a 1950s shirtwaist dress with a bust measurement that looks ideal for you, but the waist measure seems like it might be too tight, search for a similar dress with a waist measure that allows enough ease.

Even when shopping in person, knowing your measurements saves a lot of time, effort, and potential disappointment. Some vintage shops indicate measurements on tags. Others give general size indications or no indications at all. If you take along a measuring tape and measure the hanging item to get an idea if it will fit, you eliminate much of the guess work.

WAIST LENGTH, VINTAGE SIZE TYPES, AND YOUR UNIQUE FIT NEEDS

IF YOU'VE EVER TRIED on a vintage dress that, judging by its measurements, ought to fit your waist with the ease you need for comfort, but instead it was too tight, you have probably experienced a length problem. For items with a fitted bodice, having your own back waist length coincide with the item's is vital.

Lengths can be a significant factor for nearly any type of garment. I recently saw a 1940s vintage size chart that defined a 5' 6" woman as "tall." Today 5' 6" might be defined as "average," since so many of us are now taller than that.

It's not only the numbers assigned to sizes that shifted throughout the twentieth century, but also size types. You will find Pre-teen, Teen, Junior Petite, Juniors, Misses Petite, Misses, Women's, and Half Size designations, among others, all differentiated by figure types, contours and lengths. The Pre-teen and Teen sizes reflected a shorter length and higher, smaller bust, while Juniors bridged from Teen to Misses figure types. Junior Petite and Misses Petite were the shorter versions of the Junior and Misses sizes. Misses was considered average in length and contours. Half Size was shorter, narrower at the shoulders, but fuller figured, with a proportionately larger waist than the Misses sizes. Women's sizes were for a woman of the same height as Misses, but fuller overall, including longer back waist lengths, to accommodate a fuller back.

If you see PT or T after a number, those are Pre-teen and Teen sizes; Juniors was (and still is) known by its odd number sizing. Half sizes are designated by ½ added to a number. Women's sizes started out correlating to bust size—so size 40 meant a 40" bust—but gradually became disconnected; by the 1960s you might see a size 40 with a 44" bust.

A woman of any age could wear a Junior size if that was her proportion, although clothing was often designed to suit the "average" buyer of the size.

If you are particularly tall, you may have a challenge finding a fitted vintage dress with lengths to match your own. There are vintage Tall sizes out there to be found, but these are not common. Separates are a great choice for you, and you can get a very dressy look with a skirt and matching blouse or a skirt and beautifully embellished sweater or jacket. Of course, less-fitted styles make length and size matching much easier. 1970s pants and maxi dresses were often very long from waist to hem—designed that way to wear with those groovy platform shoes!

If you are petite you are really in luck with vintage—many of the "average" vintage sizes are on the shorter side and are very likely to fit you well.

Take into account whatever fit issues you have with modern clothing and pay close attention to the corresponding measurement in vintage clothing. I have slightly broad shoulders and, from years of breathing deeply to play a horn, I have a relatively wide rib cage. You can be sure I check the under-bust measurement of any really fitted dress!

'60s CHEONGSAM OR QI PAO, A STYLE OF DRESS WITH FIT GALORE. VIVA VINTAGE CLOTHING RIGHTFULLY GAVE LOTS AND LOTS OF MEASUREMENTS FOR YOU TO CONSIDER.

Advanced fit: Vintage underpinnings

WE ARE NOW ON to more advanced aspects of fit. Fitted women's clothing of the past, at least up to the 1970s, has distinct shaping that sometimes seems unlike the human form. If you've ever encountered an impossibly small waist on a 1950s suit or impossibly high darts on a 1960s dress, you might have wondered what sort of person could wear these items.

Your very own mother and grandmother might have worn them—with the help of the arsenal of foundation garments that aided whatever was the in-vogue silhouette of a given era.

1936 ADVERTISEMENT—YOU CAN SEE HOW THIS SHAPING COULD HELP ACHIEVE THE LONG LEAN LOOK OF THE '30s. (SOURCE LIBRARY OF CONGRESS)

Vintage foundations are really different from most of the shapewear that we see today; the control and shaping were much more powerful and specific to their era, particularly in the decades around the mid-twentieth century and of course the Victorian and Edwardian eras.

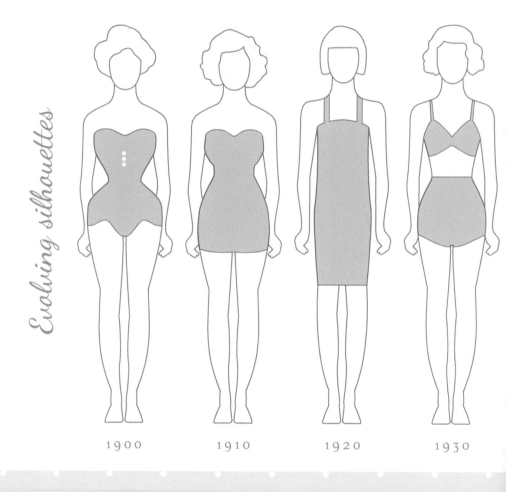

Evolving silhouettes

1900   1910   1920   1930

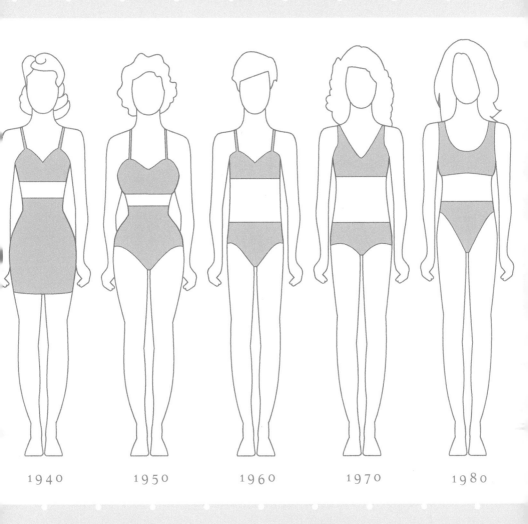

1940   1950   1960   1970   1980

The characteristic S-bend silhouette at the beginning of the twentieth century was achieved by corsets that were notoriously unhealthy for the women wearing them, and they were soon eclipsed by the WWI-era lifestyles, jobs, and fashions that demanded more freedom and less constricting control.

The 1920s ideal was slim and youthful, ideally unrestricted by underpinnings, but the hips and breasts could be downplayed by corsetry if you were not as boyishly straight as fashions insisted you be.

Elastic fabrics, particularly Lastex (invented in 1929), gave foundations sleek control under the figure-hugging silhouettes of the 1930s. The zipper was another modern innovation that improved the ease of wearing foundation garments.

During WWII, with economies around the world shifted toward war production, and women working in unparalleled numbers, undergarments became more functional. The support offered by foundation garments was seen as crucial to women's endurance in manufacturing jobs.

Dior's New Look (1947) reinvented a fancifully corseted wasp-waisted silhouette with padded hips and petticoats, followed by bust-enhancing padded bras by the early 1950s. Stretch fabrics became more and more sophisticated.

Separate girdles and bras were adopted by young women in the 1950s, part of the flowering youth culture that eventually did away with all restrictive underpinnings in the 1960s. The introduction of Spandex in 1959 transfigured the foundation industry yet again, with firm control finally both easy-care and light.

While older women were often true to the types of underpinnings they had relied on in their youth, young women in the 1970s adopted sleek and minimal control. By the late 1970s, punk style included archaic corsetry that surfaced as outerwear in a way never seen before, influencing mainstream fashion into the 1980s.

Perhaps it is easier to imagine fitting into some of the more exacting silhouettes of the twentieth century when you consider temporarily reshaping yourself with the help of underpinnings. If the vintage look you are after displays a silhouette that is natural for you, you are in luck. If you need some assistance and exercise alone can't get you, say, the waspish waist of the 1950s dresses you love, you can consider reshaping—either of the garment or yourself.

Can a structured shaper be vintage and still serve its purpose? It can, but there is a caveat. If you are able to find a powerfully controlling vintage foundation that is unused or lightly used, it is more likely to still have ample flexibility and stretch.

Alternatively, you can find quality vintage-style shapewear made in the U.S. by Rago, available online from American Shapewear. Rago was founded in 1945 and has weathered ups and downs in public demand to the present. The styles available currently could help with a range of vintage silhouettes. Another option is What Katie Did (whatkatiedid.com), which creates its lovely and functional vintage-inspired corsets, girdles, and other lingerie in the UK.

On a personal note: I do not wear vintage foundations except on special occasions and for some particular styles (for me, a 1950s sheath dress often demands smoothing over the hip). I favor clothing that doesn't demand an extreme fit; I prefer a more accommodating silhouette. One of the reasons I'm fond of early to mid-'40s clothing is that it is a more natural silhouette, one that tends to fit me. Others swear by vintage foundation wear for the way it makes their clothes fit, makes their clothes look, and makes them feel. Some believe you can't really have the whole vibe of the past without the structure that our predecessors endured or enjoyed, as the case may be. I think this is a personal decision. I don't consider it *wrong* to skip the vintage under-structure, but it is important to understand how it impacted fit and how you might be able to wear something you love with just a bit of undercover help. Perhaps there was and is tyranny in insisting that women's bodies be shaped for fashion, but perhaps there is also tyranny in insisting that they not be. Let it be up to you.

It would be a slip up not to mention slips. Many vintage dresses and blouses are sheer or semi-sheer and the expectation was that the wearer would be wearing a slip or camisole underneath. Some dresses came with their own slips, but many didn't. Your choice of slip can whimsically vary the look of the dress—picture a bright red slip under a navy eyelet dress, for example. Vintage slips, often beautifully trimmed, can be found in a range of colors, fabrics, and lengths. I personally keep a bevy of vintage slips and half slips, along with a couple of petticoats (crinolines) for the 1950s skirts that seem to beg for loft.

DEBBIE REYNOLDS, 1953 (PHOTO EVERETT COLLECTION)

Obviously, besides its dutiful shaping and layering, glamour and allure are among vintage lingerie's greatest charms.

J. ROUSSEL PARIS ADVERTISEMENT, 1947

A little about alterations

BECAUSE MUCH of the new clothing available now is inexpensive and only briefly fashionable—not to mention stretchy and without structure—most people purchase clothes without thinking about an exacting fit. The one exception might be for a wedding, when there is a scramble to find an alterations expert. In our parents' and grandparents' times, alterations were done routinely. Almost nothing was a perfect fit right off the rack, nor was it expected to be. A woman might have the skills herself to make it fit or have a relative or friend to do the work; otherwise, it was off to the seamstress, with whom one might develop a strong bond—she would know what worked best for her individual clients and make astute suggestions.

Since vintage clothing is often more fitted than modern clothing, the alterations expert is still an absolutely invaluable resource, and more than just for weddings!

For those who are wondering if Yves Saint Laurent would turn in his grave if you were to alter a nice vintage piece, know that at least 20% of vintage clothing probably has been altered already, most likely to fit the original owner. I believe it is fine to alter an item to fit you, as long as you keep the integrity of its design. On the other hand, there are those who are pretty drastic in what they do to nice vintage pieces, and to them I'd say there is a distinct difference between altering and ransacking. Cutting a vintage dress right through hand-stitched embroidery to make it 10" shorter, for instance, is butchery, not alteration. I believe in leaving a sheath a sheath and a shift a shift, making alterations for fit while keeping the cut of the original.

There is one sort of creative revamping that definitely makes sense: A seamstress may be able to save a vintage item that has been damaged, should you find one that has much that is right about it. I had a dress that had quite a few holes in its skirt. With a beautiful rhinestone-encrusted neckline and back pleats, I didn't want to sideline the dress completely so I brought it to my excellent seamstress. She was able to make a peplum tunic while taking all the damaged parts away.

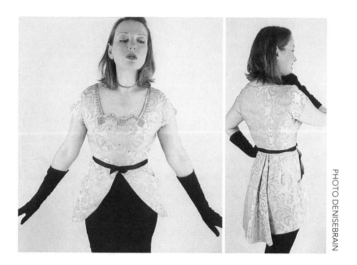

It's definitely *not* butchery to have a slightly-too-large piece made perfect for you. Taking a fitted waist in or out may involve small changes to side seams, darts, or pleats. If your pants drag on the ground when you are wearing the shoes you plan to wear with them, by all means, hem them up.

An item is worth altering if it is something you love and it doesn't quite fit you well. I guarantee you will love it more when it fits!

A few tips for responsible and successful altering:

- If possible, leave all the extra fabric of the inseams and hem intact in an alteration so that the piece can be altered back again.

- The fewer changes you make, the less expensive the alteration will be, so if economy is important to you, choose something that just needs one or maybe two minor changes.

- A terribly rare or extremely valuable item is probably best to preserve as it is.

- It is easier (and usually less expensive) to make something a bit smaller than a bit larger.

- Although some seam allowances are large enough to let out, the fabric can sometimes show the previous stitching line.

- If the condition of the garment isn't sturdy, it probably won't be worth altering.

An alterations expert can also mend and repair a garment for you. If replacing a zipper, fixing a torn buttonhole, or restoring a hem are not skills you possess, you'll need to find a seamstress.

How do you find a skilled seamstress? How much should alterations cost?

These are hard questions to answer in any concrete way, because your town may differ from Paris or New York or Charlotte or Fargo—you do need to find someone locally. If there are vintage clothing shops in your area, you might ask the owners if they have any recommendations (some may even have alterations people who come in regularly). If you know anyone who wears vintage, ask if she has a recommendation. If you have a trusted dry cleaner, inquire there. Look in the phone book and online. Ask on Facebook or Twitter. Inquire at a local fabric shop or sewing school. Once you have someone in mind, take a test item, one that you wouldn't cry over if it were lost. If it comes out great, and you liked the seamstress, you can feel safe taking more items. I especially appreciate a seamstress who loves and respects vintage clothing, which they frequently do because they are interested in the fine points of clothing construction often seen in vintage items.

Tailor vs. seamstress, what's the difference? Both tailors and seamstresses probably will be able to help you with your vintage clothing needs. "Tailor" is the traditional term for a male professional who can create a suit or coat from scratch or do alterations. "Seamstress" is the traditional term for a female professional who sews for a living, whether simply sewing side seams in a garment factory or as a highly skilled dressmaker. Oh, and yes, there are women tailors and men seamsters!

Reweaving is a specialized skill for repairing small holes in garments. The process involves collecting threads from inconspicuous places in a damaged item, using these to hand weave horizontally and vertically across the hole, making it close to invisible. The more textured the fabric, the more successful this is likely to be, although a very skilled reweaver can work miracles even on smoother fabrics. Ask seamstresses, tailors, and dry cleaners who does reweaving in your area. These specialists are getting rarer, and I believe in supporting those who undertake it, keeping their skill—and our vintage finery—alive.

Condition of vintage items: What to look for

IF YOU ARE NOT SHOPPING at a brick and mortar store where you can assess in person, you will need to look carefully at the described condition and photos of any vintage fashion item you are interested in, including every detail about flaws. Love at first sight is all well and good, but if a vintage dress is starting to fall apart, or if a vintage swimsuit is missing its elastic, your love may go unrequited—your clothes may go unworn.

For a beginning buyer of vintage online, I recommend concentrating on items that are described as being in excellent condition. In most cases, excellent is the best condition you will find, the only thing better is mint, but mint condition is rare. You might assume that never-worn vintage clothing is always a good bet, but never-worn or unused is not the same as mint condition; sometimes age has taken a toll even on unused items. Other terms you'll come across for never-worn vintage clothing include: deadstock, with tags, virgin, or NOS (new old stock).

Whether used or unused, if something is described as being in excellent condition, it should have no real flaws, or flaws that are so small that they don't call attention to themselves at all. You may have seen a vintage item described as being in good condition, or very good condition, and wondered what that meant. I mean, isn't *good* perfectly *fine*? Years ago, a group of online vintage sellers hammered out a set of terms to codify condition ratings. This chart has been edited and refined by various groups and sellers:

CONDITION CHART

Mint – as new with absolutely no flaws or wear

Excellent – used with no noticeable flaws

Very Good – used with minor flaws, no repairs needed

Good – visible wear, minor flaws and/or optional repairs needed

Fair – numerous flaws, repairs needed, fragile

Poor – extensive damage—for display or study use only

Noting the flaws in each piece is a big job for a seller, but it is the only way for an online buyer to gain a sense of any potential issues. Although not all online vintage shops show a chart like this, its creation codified the language used by online vintage sellers; its terms are prevalent. Chart or no chart, these exact words or others similar, what matters most are the details of the condition, shown and described. The issues need to be enumerated.

You will see the term "vintage condition" in many clothing descriptions; it is often used by vintage sellers to mean something like "good considering its age." I don't use the term because it kind of muddies the waters—in reality, vintage items can be good as new or in excellent condition without further qualification.

To be honest, for non-formal occasions I personally wear plenty of vintage items with some flaws. If you love the item and know you look and feel good in it, the flaws will likely be minor for you. It takes a little experience with vintage to know how far you are able to go with condition issues. Start with very small problems (worn cuffs, mismatched buttons, or a tiny hole for instance) and discover your personal tolerance.

I DIDN'T WANT TO SELL THIS 1940s DRESS DUE TO A HANDFUL OF TINY HOLES, BUT I WEAR IT HAPPILY MYSELF BECAUSE THE PRINT DISGUISES THE HOLES PRETTY WELL. WITH EXPERIENCE YOU CAN FIGURE OUT WHAT YOU CAN FIX AND WHAT YOU CAN PUT UP WITH. (PHOTO DENISEBRAIN)

A bargain price on an amazing-looking item may reflect serious problems. If a seller rates the condition anything less than mint or excellent and doesn't describe the flaws, ask. The seller needs to describe (and ideally also show) what keeps the item from having excellent or mint status.

I have purchased items and discovered they had flaws that the sellers didn't adequately describe but that I'm sure they saw, like gaping holes in the lining. Remember that as a buyer you do not need to accept items if their condition is not as described—

unless the seller specifically states that the item is sold "as is" and that there are no refunds. You have to get in the habit of reading a seller's terms of sale. If you are looking at an item from a seller you trust, you may not need to question what "very good" means, but if someone you don't know says something is in very good condition without explanation, I would ask for more detail. For pieces described as being in good condition, even more so. If you're not careful, you may end up with the proverbial hole with a sweater around it!

At this point it must be obvious how important it is to look at the online seller's reputation. On websites like Etsy and eBay, buyer feedback and reviews are major factors in a seller's repute. Many stand-alone vintage fashion websites include testimonials, and you can also research the vendor to see if they have been mentioned online. Social media posts by—and interactions with—the seller can give you the flavor of their character. Almost every seller who has been around for a while has gotten a less-than-stellar review here and there, but if there are problems that crop up repeatedly in reviews, take those into account.

Again, take the time to read a seller's terms of sale; many vintage sellers do not accept returns, or they accept returns only if they have made a big error in describing an item. At a time when people are used to purchasing online, then returning items for any reason, this may seem like a hardship, but think about it: A small business that offers one-of-a-kind vintage items does not have the same business structure as a large retailer and is probably not netting anything close to the same profit. Purchasing vintage is a two-way street, with accuracy and detail required from the seller, and care and knowledge required from the buyer.

Which online dealers are recommended? There are a lot of lists out there, and I can't possibly name each and every great vintage vendor. Some are best known for mod '60s fashions, others for war-era '40s; some specialize in hats, others in swimwear. Look for the sellers with great reputations who sell fashion that you routinely crush on.

As a member of the Vintage Fashion Guild (vintagefashionguild. org), I can vouch for the reputations of the other Guild members. The group vets its members for accuracy, integrity, and professionalism, so although one certainly doesn't need to be a member be an excellent, reputable vintage seller, I believe you won't go wrong with a VFG seller. You can find a list of the member sellers on the Vintage Fashion Guild website.

Taking care of your vintage finery

THERE IS A LOT to be known about caring for vintage fashions, from simple mending to the curatorial processes of museums. Much of the basic care is similar to that which you'd use with modern clothing, although more and more of us are getting away from such basic knowledge as how to hand wash clothing or iron a shirt. You may be new to caring for your wearables *and* new to vintage, and I don't want you to feel overwhelmed. For that reason, I have tried to hone this category to just the most reliable care methods, the methods I would want to know if I were starting out myself right now. Chances are you know some of this, and can just skim through, but if you aren't familiar, or have not had much success, I hope this chapter will give you some ideas. This section might also help to explain why something that has failed to work for you in the past really can't be done.

If this chapter has a lot that's new to you, please know that I've been where you are. I wasn't born into a household with a mentor even remotely resembling a Martha Stewart. I learned to sew and wash garments, but the intricacies were unknown to me. When I got started with vintage, I did a lot of research and experimentation.

I have what looks like a small chemistry lab in my home, with every sort of product that has been extolled for cleaning, and odor-, and spot-removing. I have two sewing machines and several rainbows of thread. I have drawers filled with braids, laces, buttons sorted by color, replacement fasteners, bias and hem tapes, appliqués, elastic, zippers, rhinestones in all sizes and colors, sequins, beads, paillettes, and every other spangle imaginable. I have a library of books on mending and cleaning.

In other words, I have tried a lot of things, and I want to give you just the very best and simplest of my most successful processes for taking care of vintage.

PREVENTION

I CAN'T SAY it enough: Start by choosing vintage items that don't have flaws, or have only minor flaws, then wear the clothing thoughtfully. It is so much easier to wear and preserve something in great shape, then gradually advance your garment care know-how as needed.

Before you buy

One very big damage prevention measure is to make sure the vintage item is likely to fit before putting it on in the first place (see "Figuring out vintage fit and size" on page 55). Wearing clothing that is too tight risks tears, seam breaks, and disappointment.

Consider the condition carefully, looking for something you don't have to immediately research spot removers for or mend.

Before and during wearings

Choose jewelry carefully. In selecting a brooch, for instance, make sure it has a very fine, sharp pin if you are going to poke it through fine fabric. I like to test the pin on an inconspicuous place to see how the pinhole will look on the fabric.

I've seen a lot of dust, puddle stains, and heel tears at the hems of long dresses. Excessive length ought to be hemmed up, and a little lifting of trains and hems will help avoid damage.

Take care not to spill while eating, and don't overdo the fence climbing, Charleston dancing, corsage pinning, and puddle splashing. Hang up your clothing even if it is sweaty or dirty and you intend to clean it. When your clothing needs cleaning, do so as soon as you can after wearing it.

Champagne and soda may appear clear, but the sugar in these drinks oxidizes with heat over time, and develops into a brown stain. Make sure you wash or clean a garment after spilling drinks. It isn't coffee or tea that has done in many a wedding gown, but champagne.

Many times I've felt like sending up a hallelujah when I have found dress shields sewn into vintage clothes. Dress shields are underarm liners that protect a blouse or dress from perspiration and stains from deodorants. Shields can be attached to the garment or they might have bands that hold them in place on you, and/or your bra. You can find disposable shields, but we vintage people are into reusable, right? My favorites are by the same brand that I find in vintage dresses, Kleinert's, which has been in the business since 1869.

Between wearings: Storing vintage clothing

Two giant don'ts: plastic bags and wire hangers.

Remember Faye Dunaway as Joan Crawford in *Mommie Dearest*? "NO...WIRE...HANGERS. What's wire hangers doing in this closet when I told you no wire hangers EVER!?"

Those wire hangers can go back to most dry cleaners for reuse, but do NOT store your clothes hanging on them. They can stretch and tear your garments' shoulders, the hooks can catch on clothes, and eventually they will even leave rust stains.

Wood hangers are handsome, but I can't recommend them for your vintage clothes because wood (and some of the stains and finishes used on wooden hangers) can react with and damage fabric.

Padded hangers are friendliest to vintage clothing that can be hung, with the weight of the garment distributed over the shoulders. The padding will also help enforce some space in your closet, so that wrinkles don't develop, and fabrics have a bit of room to breathe. You can make your own padded hangers by wrapping plastic hangers in batting and plain cotton muslin.

Many a vintage gown has a pair of inner ribbons to loop over the center of the hanger to take the weight of the dress off the shoulders and straps, and to prevent the dress from slipping off the hanger. Use these.

I find that typical skirt and pants hangers, the kinds with those pinching clips, can put permanent dents in fabric, so I turn the garment inside out to clip the reverse side, and often also distribute the pressure of the clip with padding. Some skirts and pants have inner loops for hanging, much like dresses.

Some things are best not hung at all. Have you ever put on a mini-length knit dress only to find it had become a midi? Welcome to the world of gravity! When you go to store your knits, it is best to fold or roll them and set them on shelves.

Not that this is beginner's stuff, but if you have a heavy and delicate, fragile, or very vintage garment (such as a beaded silk dress from the 1920s) do not hang it at all, but let it rest flat, or softly roll it padded with acid-free tissue paper. For that type of precious garment, you will also want to invest in acid-free boxes for storage.

(Cue the Joan Crawford voice again.) Do *not* store garments in dry cleaning bags or garment bags made of plastic or vinyl. Plastic doesn't breathe and can trap moisture that nurtures mold and mildew. Over time, plastic can react with fabric and break down. I have seen and felt plastic garment bags that literally adhered to the vintage clothes stored inside them. Cotton muslin garment bags (or simply covering the clothes with old cotton sheets) can help keep stored vintage clothing clean and protected against potential damage from closet mates. Tyvek®, used for making garment bags, is another possibility. It is pH neutral, acid free, and tear resistant. It also keeps water out while allowing moisture vapor to escape.

Do not store any clothing (vintage or new) in sunlight for any length of time. I have seen a printed cotton robe fade within several days of being placed near a window, so it sometimes doesn't take long. You might actually have a window in your closet, and this will need to be curtained or shaded. You might hang a gorgeous vintage kimono or evening gown up for display on a wall, but be careful that sunlight doesn't hit that wall. I'm fortunate that my outdoor laundry line runs through both shade and sun—I can use the sunlight for fading and bleaching. Incandescent light, although much less potent than UV light, can also fade fabric over time. Fluorescent, compact fluorescent, and LED lights are considerably less harmful to fabric.

Avoid storing clothing in extreme temperatures and/or humidity. Moisture is particularly damaging to fabric. The rule is that your vintage clothing is going to be comfortable if *you* are, kept at 65–75 degrees Fahrenheit and about 40–50% humidity. Dehumidifiers come in a range from inexpensive disposable moisture-absorbing pellets to rather costly (but effective and long-lasting) appliances. Basements and attics can have drastic temperature swings that damage fabric, and basements in particular can be damp. Which reminds me: Avoid mildew (and even dye transfer) by waiting until a garment is completely dry after washing, before hanging it in a closet.

Various climates pose various challenges. You can have a bone-dry, dusty environment in the desert, or a hot and humid environment in the lower latitudes. The same kind of air conditioning that makes you comfortable, will make your clothes happy too.

Hang up your vintage clothing even if it needs cleaning, and don't wait long to clean it. If there are obvious stains, the sooner you try to get them out, the better—and keep in mind that many stains appear only over time. It's a good practice to keep the area surrounding your vintage clothing clean so there's less chance of attracting fabric-eating pests.

Keeping fabric-eating insects at bay

Insects. I know, ewww, right?

But did you know that clothes moths (and other fabric munchers) serve a useful purpose? In their natural (outdoor) setting, they are scavengers, breaking down feathers, fur, skin, and other cast-off organic ingredients that then become part of the soil. That's right, the little varmints don't specifically want to eat your best cashmere sweater, but if stuck inside, they will make do with it.

OK, enough with the niceties, let's get down to business.

Many of our foremothers' vintage ways are well worth reviving, but one that is not is the use of dangerous pesticides to kill fabric-eating pests. You really get a sense of desperation from the packaging of these products!

MICHIGAN STATE UNIVERSITY ARCHIVES & HISTORICAL COLLECTIONS

A little bit about the major fabric-eating insects:

1. **Carpet beetles** are very small (⅛" to ³⁄₁₆" [.32 to .48 cm]) flying insects. There are a number of species of carpet beetles, each with different but similar markings. The adult carpet beetle is not harmful to fabric, but its larvae will eat fur, hair, feathers, silk, wool, mohair, cashmere, or any other hair fiber. This is the only insect I have experience trying to control. I found that the adults love light and white surfaces and can be spotted on windowsills and light fixtures. The dark-preferring larvae are like tiny (¼" [.64 cm] long) caterpillars. They are hairy and yellowish to gold to black-brown, depending upon the species. The larvae of course do not fly, but hatch from eggs and get to work on eating your clothing.

2. **Clothes moths** are of two types: Webbing clothes moths, which are the most common in the U.S., and case-bearing clothes moths. Both species produce very short-lived adults, the webbing type is gold/buff in color and has a wing span of about ½" (1.27 cm) while the case-bearing variety is even smaller. They are at home in dark places and perfectly content to live in your closet. Again, it's the larvae that do the damage, and these love to eat the same things as the carpet beetle: Woolens, hair, fur, hair fibers, silk, and feathers. The tiny (up to ½" [1.27 cm]), worm-like larvae of the webbing moth is distinct from the case-bearing moth's larvae, which forms a silken mantle that can be white, or colored with the tints of what it is eating, making them harder to see. Soiling of your stored clothing is what attracts the moth; vitamin B from sources such as sweat and body oil serves as food for the earliest stage of the larvae, without which it can't survive.

3. **Silverfish and firebrats** are nocturnal, wingless insects that thrive in moist, warm environments. Silverfish like temperatures in the 70s and 80s, while the firebrat likes 90+ degrees, such as you might find in an attic. The ¼" to ½" (.64 to 1.27 cm) long adults eat a wide-ranging menu—especially oriented toward anything with protein, sugar, and starch—including book bindings and paper, wall paper (for the paste), carpeting, clothing, coffee, hair, some paints, photos, plaster, glue, and sugar. They will eat any starched fabric such as cotton and linen, along with wool, rayon, silk, fur, feathers, and even leather.

With the thought of your vintage cashmere coat's nap being mowed down by one of these pests, and the prospect of sprinkling poisons around to kill them, I think we can agree that an ounce of prevention is worth a ton of cure.

I am very fortunate to live in a dry environment with hard freezes during the winters. Insect infestations are not the problem that they can be elsewhere. For those not so lucky, it may always be necessary to thoroughly clean or freeze or heat (instructions upcoming) vintage finds. Launder any new-to-you sturdy, washable vintage item, or have it dry cleaned if that is what is best for the item.

Keep your home and especially your clothing storage area clean and dry. Vacuum the nooks and crannies. Fabric-eating insects are attracted by animal hair, sweat, body oils, and food. Don't store clothes that need cleaning because those are invitations to pests. Avoid using starch on your clothing, which also attracts insects. Keep a vigilant eye on your stored items to make sure no new infestation has started. Don't forget your handbags and shoes can attract these critters as well, and should be kept as clean as possible. Some insects (crickets, cockroaches, termites) are attracted to food and other stains on your clothing, and although they don't eat the fabric, they can cut through it while eating their meal. There are so many excellent reasons to keep your clothes clean—this just might be the *most* compelling of them all!

Dry cleaning kills pests and removes stains that attract them. Washing to remove stains on a garment will make the clothing uninteresting to pests. Keeping your vintage finery clean is your first line of defense.

Use is a perfect deterrent for insect pests. As long as you keep wearing your clothing it is not going to be possible for an infestation to take hold. Of course, you can't wear that mohair sweater in the middle of summer—most of us have to find a safe way to store our clothes.

Freezing is used to kill insect pests, but it will only work if your home freezer goes down to -20°F (-28.9°C)—and you have space in it! Freezing under these very cold conditions will work well to kill adults, larvae, and eggs of insects. To freeze an item, seal it in a plastic bag and give it three days in your freezer. When you take it out, be careful; in a frozen state the item will be more brittle. Let your item rest in its bag for another 24 hours, allowing it to acclimate again to room temperature. Allow any condensation to evaporate before you store your garment again. If you get your timing right, and if you live where the temperature dips low enough, you might be able to put a batch of clothing outside during a deep freeze.

I have read about lavender being an insect deterrent. Apparently, as lovely as its scent is to *us*, it may discourage adult fabric-eating insects. I'd say go ahead and use it so your closet and drawers smell good, but don't expect it to kill anything, or stop the larvae from feeding on your items.

According to MuseumPests.net, cedar does not work as an insect repellant. Although cedar oil can kill the earliest stage of clothes moth larvae, it does not kill the eggs, the adult moths, or other pests. If your great aunt had good experiences with keeping her sweaters in a cedar chest, it might just have been the sealed-off conditions that helped the most. Storage is best achieved in a plastic bin with a tightly fitting lid. Your clean clothing should be wrapped in plain cotton to help absorb moisture in the bin. Plastic is not good for fabric over the long haul, but storage for several months is fine, like the several months during which you wouldn't use your sweaters over the summer.

Heat may also be used to kill insects in all life stages. Using an oven's warm setting, which is usually 140°F (60°C—do *not* use higher heat), place your clothing item on a clean, oven-proof tray or sheet pan on a rack with a pan of water on a lower rack. After three hours of "cooking," turn the oven off, removing the item when it has cooled down. Carefully controlled heat is even used by exterminators for safely killing pest infestations in entire hotels. It truly does work.

There are readily available non-toxic pheromone traps that attract adult males of specific insect species. These work to help you identify the critter involved in an infestation, and eventually break the cycle of damage, but they do not help isolate the larvae that do the damage in the first place. If you are really stuck with a terrible infestation after doing all you can to keep your vintage safe, I would recommend hiring a professional exterminator.

One last thing. I have come to appreciate the help of spiders (as long as there aren't TOO many) in my house. They eat these pesky fabric-munching insects with relish, and probably are much more capable of finding some of the hiding places in your floorboards and carpets than you are.

OK, one LAST last thing: If there was such a vote, I'd be chosen Least Likely to Vacuum Every Nook and Cranny. I'm not incredibly fastidious, but I'm very fortunate to live where insects just aren't the problem that they are in other regions. The one time I found my absolute favorite cashmere sweater riddled with holes, I learned just how much others suffer with insect damage. That's when I looked up everything there is to know about controlling carpet beetles. It's not a pleasant subject, but it is one about which to have some knowledge if you want to protect the clothing that you not only invested in, but love.

MANY OF THE SAME clothing care and storage guidelines apply to accessories, but there are special considerations based on their shape and material.

Hats. Hat boxes are not only attractive but (surprise, surprise!) very useful for storing your vintage hats, although other boxes will also work fine. Usually, a bit of carefully placed acid-free tissue paper can protect hats stored together in a box, and will protect a hat from a non-acid-free box over time. You can cradle delicate features such as feather plumes with

COURTESY OF KASEY BUICK

tissue "nests." If you have just a few hats or want to show off a few, and they are sufficiently sturdy, by all means place them on shelves or wig stands. Just keep them out of direct light and give them a dusting from time to time. For dusting and cleaning hats, two interesting tools to have on hand are canned air and a soft paintbrush. You can also work with a hair dryer on its cool setting and any soft-bristled brush. A steamer can help make a warped brim pliable enough to reshape, straighten a crumpled veil, and fluff up a flattened flower.

Veils can be particularly delicate and vulnerable, and I store veiled hats with their veils gently tucked inside, tissue separating the netting from the hat if there are any rough spots.

Many vintage hats are made of wool felt, vulnerable to insect damage, so take care to keep your hats away from critters.

Bag storage. Many a very respectable vintage handbag has been ruined by being stacked in a pile, with the surface and structure creased, dented or even broken down. The best way to store bags is sitting upright on a shelf, and if the structure needs to be bolstered, stuff the bag with a clean old cotton t-shirt, a chunk of unbleached cotton, or a wad of crumpled acid-free tissue paper.

Bags are notorious for the odors they transport through the decades, from cigarette smoke to perfume. For the newcomer to vintage, I absolutely recommend choosing a bag with no odors. Stuffing the bag with tissue which is periodically replaced can help remove mild odors. Using Zero Odor (more about this product under "Odor removal tips" [page 108]) and leaving the bag open to air out can help. I have used dryer sheets in bags with stronger odors, but, of course, one ends up with the dryer sheet's perfume-y odor that also lingers.

PHOTO LAUREN NAIMOLA,
DEAR GOLDEN

Shoe storage. For short-term storage (about 18 months), a shoe rack or placement on a shelf is just fine, but for longer storage it's best to box vintage shoes and use acid-free tissue as stuffing to support their shape. Take care not to overstuff or you can stretch the shoes. Wrap the shoes individually in more tissue or plain cotton and set them in a box. Moisture can promote mildew, so use a breathable card-board box, preferably acid-free for your most cherished shoes. You can find acid-free photo boxes in just the right size for a pair of shoes.

Bag and shoe care. Leather can and should be cleaned and conditioned. I like Cadillac Leather Lotion, which helps to preserve leather, reptile skins, and also imitation leather surfaces. You can use it on your shoes, bags, and even jackets. There are many other products that work similarly, such as saddle soap. For smooth leather (not napped, suede, or glove leather) that has become dry, use a leather conditioner. I like Lexol.

Suede can be brushed with a suede brush or rough towel. It is not as sturdy as smooth leather, and it will easily absorb dirt, moisture, and oils. If you have a small, dry stain to remove from suede, you can start by softly scrubbing it with a cloth or art gum eraser. Be gentle and don't dig a hole in the suede's nap, but do loosen the stain, and raise the nap that might have been stuck down with the stain.

You can use a vacuum cleaner to clean the interiors of bags and shoes, and to remove dust from the exterior of sturdy fabric bags and shoes that don't have beading or other potentially loose embellishments. For those vulnerable ones, use a screen over the head of your vacuum wand, or use a soft brush to loosen and sweep away dirt.

Patent leather (real or faux) can be cared for with some common household products. You can wash the surface with a damp cloth. A glass cleaner can be used to remove dirt and improve the shine. Use a soft cloth with petroleum jelly or mineral oil to rub out scuffs and then use the cloth to polish the remainder of the shoe or purse. Use a clean cloth to buff to a shine. If you have a stubborn scuff or fogging, first try rubbing it with isopropyl alcohol on a cotton swab. If that doesn't do the trick, using a low percentage acetone (the kind used for fingernail polish remover) with a cotton swab may work. Follow up with mineral oil or petroleum jelly to help restore the gloss. With the acetone you'll be removing some of the protective lacquer, so use it with caution.

If your shoes' insoles have lifted around the edges, I would recommend using a shoe glue such as Shoe Goo or Barge Cement. Use a paintbrush to help apply the glue. If the insole seems to be coming loose, you might want to carefully lift it off and reglue it entirely.

Just like finding a good dry cleaner and seamstress, it is a very good idea to find a good shoe repair shop, one that respects vintage workmanship. Replacing soles and heel tips, stitching, and dyeing are all things that can be done by a good shoe repair person.

Scarves. Collecting scarves can be addictive, and if you have considerably more than can be reasonably stacked or rolled in a drawer, consider a hanging set of loops. These can be made of any kind of plastic, so long as they don't have any rough spots. The added advantage of this hanging method is being able to see them all better.

Almost all scarves, even those made of silk, can be hand washed, using cool to tepid water and very mild soap or baby shampoo. You may see some dye bleed, but if you don't leave the scarf to soak too long (or wash more than one at a time) you will be fine. If you have stains to remove, you can try using the mild soap on the spot as a pretreatment, first checking on a tiny bit of an edge of the scarf to make sure the color doesn't fade noticeably with the full-strength soap. Don't wring or twist, but roll the washed and rinsed scarf in a clean towel before laying it flat to dry. You can then iron it using a press cloth and a low heat setting just as it reaches a nearly dry stage. Avoid ironing on a rolled (hand-sewn) hem to preserve its soft, dimensional look. If a silk scarf has lost its gloss, you can sometimes bring some of that back by rinsing it in a solution of white vinegar and water (¼ cup per gallon).

Gloves. In our mother's and grandmother's days, gloves were often stored in pretty, decorative long boxes. I have so many gloves that I keep them in boxes by color, with one small drawer devoted to long white gloves, and one to short white gloves.

The vintage way of washing gloves is to leave them on and proceed as if you are washing your hands, using a gentle soap and lukewarm water. You can use a soft brush for spots. Invert the gloves and repeat the hand washing, then rinse them thoroughly. Allow the gloves to dry away from heat. Keep colorful gloves away from their white and cream counterparts to avoid dye bleed.

If you have unlined leather gloves that are clearly stamped "washable" inside, you should be able to wash them by hand successfully using the same technique, but with a couple of additional steps. Roll the washed gloves in a towel from the fingertips to the cuffs, allowing water to drain from the cuffs. When the gloves are nearly dry, put them on, allowing them to shape again to your hands. If they have already dried completely, moistening your hands before pulling them on will help to get the shape back. If the gloves are not clearly marked washable, they haven't been tanned to allow washing and would need to be dry cleaned. Dry cleaning washable leather gloves negates the option of washing them. Any dry cleaned or non-washable leather gloves will shrink badly if washed.

After all, you want them to fit like a glove–not smaller!

FABRICS 101

ONE OF THE THINGS I am most frequently asked is how a particular vintage garment should be cleaned. The answer to that involves at least a little understanding of fabrics. Knowing a bit about fabrics will help in other ways too, because it will tell you a lot about a garment that you are looking at online–the way it will feel, drape, and stretch, as well as how to maintain it. It will also help you to assess the price. If you are like me you will soon have favorite fabrics, ones that you seek out over others.

Vintage clothing dealers have different levels of knowledge about fabric. Although most will do what they can to specify the fabric of an item, sometimes they may only be able to describe it as soft and smooth, or heavy and thick. These words can at least help you get a feeling for what you're purchasing.

Why does the fabric matter? Have you ever purchased a blouse that dried within 15 minutes of washing, making it great for travel? a coat that kept you toasty warm on the coldest day? a dress that had a crisp look and rustled when you walked into a party? ...or a pair of pants that looked great, but made you sweat and itch? All these characteristics have a lot to do with fabrics, and becoming familiar with them will help you make more gratifying choices.

The price of a vintage garment can also be affected by its fabric. Fine wool gabardine would make a more valuable suit than a rougher, more loosely woven wool. Knowing the difference between silk velvet, rayon velvet, and cotton velvet will help you compare their prices. Fabric savvy can also help you know what sort of investment you will need for upkeep, and will help you take good care of your vintage finery once it lives in your closet.

Before 1960, clothing rarely had any fabric content and care labeling. The Textile Products Identification Act of 1960 mandated fabric content labeling in garments. This information was usually printed on a hang tag that was removed before wearing the clothing. Our familiar sewn-in care tags were required as of 1972. This was a huge step in making clothing easier to maintain. Now, we take these tags for granted, but our foremothers had to know enough to make good washing and other care decisions themselves.

In general, don't throw vintage clothes in a washing machine for a regular wash. Clothes from the 1970s onward may be labeled to show that they are routinely machine washable, but if you would like to preserve the clothing longer, go the friendliest route, either a very gentle machine wash or hand wash (more on that to come). I can't recommend using your dryer for anything vintage.

Although my washing machine is something of a simple work-horse, I understand that there are some wonderful washing machines made now, with plenty of controls to get just the effect you might want for doing a fine job of replicating hand washing. If you have one of those machines and know it well, hooray for you and your options. A washer is a big investment, and it's always good to read unbiased reviews from Consumer Reports before taking the plunge.

Whether you are a vintage virgin, a vintage virtuoso, or somewhere in between, you might not be confident about fabric. What follows are the basics.

Fabrics are finished products woven or knit from fibers. The fibers can be natural: mainly cotton, wool, silk, and linen; or manufactured: mainly rayon, acetate, acrylic, nylon, and polyester. The most common weaves are plain, satin, and twill.

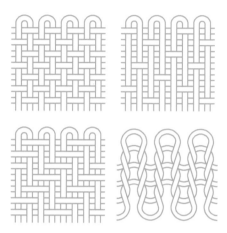

THE ANATOMY OF THE BASIC WEAVES (*LEFT TO RIGHT FROM TOP*):
PLAIN, SATIN, AND TWILL, ALONG WITH KNIT

With the exception of linen, which is the name used for both a fiber and a fabric, all other fabrics have a two-part name: One part is the fiber or fiber blend, the other is the fabric type. If you see a fabric listed as silk taffeta, you are being told that the fiber is silk, and the fabric type is taffeta. Likewise, a rayon jersey is a jersey knit fabric made of rayon fiber.

If you have a piece of vintage clothing without a fabric content label and you'd like to know what the material is made of, try the most accessible test out there: A fiber burn test. I described how to do this in detail for the Vintage Fashion Guild's *Fabric Resource* (vintagefashionguild.org/determining-fiber). The basic process involves snipping a small piece of fabric from an inseam, then carefully burning it with a lighter while observing how the fiber behaves (looks, smells, feels) during and after. You can then compare your findings to the chart on the next page.

This takes a little practice, but I guarantee it can be learned. Practice by burning snippets of fabric that you're already familiar with to get the feel for how, say, silk burns.

If you are fortunate to know such a person, you can learn about fabrics with the help of someone in the know, a fabric mentor. You can also usually get small swatches of yardage from a fabric store to get a feel (quite literally) of what fabrics are like.

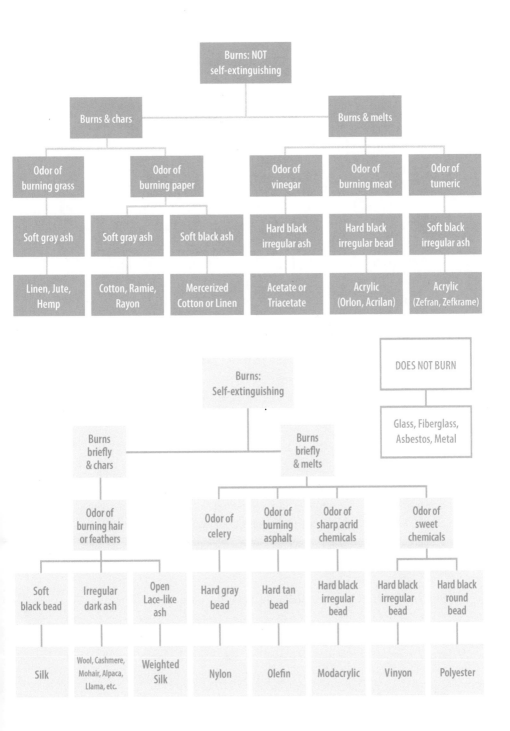

COTTON IS A FIBER obtained from the seed pods of the cotton plant. It is naturally fine, soft, fluffy, and absorbent. Fabrics made from cotton can be crisp or soft; most are easy to care for, washable in warm water, cool and comfortable to wear. The wide variety of cotton fabrics range from sheer batiste to heavy denim, and from ribbed corduroy to the interlock knit of t-shirts.

Cotton fabrics are mostly sturdy and washable in warm water with any detergent, but cotton may shrink, and its dyes and prints may fade. Some kinds of cottons have special finishes that may wash out, such as glazing or sizing. While many modern, synthetic finishes are permanent, vintage finishes made of glue, starch, resin, gelatin or paraffin may not be. Cotton is often best (crisper and smoother) when ironed, and easiest to iron while it is still slightly damp. Although you may use warm water for cotton, hot water and hot drying can cause the fibers to shrink, fade and weaken.

Should you use bleach? Chlorine bleach is hard on fabric, even sturdy cotton (it's death to other fibers). It will weaken the fibers, fade the colors, and turn any synthetic component in the fabric yellow. A non-chlorine bleach such as Oxiclean or Biz may be used on cotton, but don't use it to bathe silk or wool.

Oxiclean is the most readily available non-chlorine bleach in the U.S., but there are quite a few others. Look for the words "oxygen bleach" and make sure there is no chlorine in the ingredients. A non-chlorine bleach will have hydrogen peroxide in some form. Powdered peroxide compounds become hydrogen peroxide when they hit water, and in the case of Oxiclean, washing soda is added to raise the pH. Alkalinity helps boost the peroxide.

SILK IS OBTAINED by reeling filaments from the cocoons of silk moths. The filaments from a single cocoon of one silkworm are on average a mile long, and are strong, glossy and resilient. Made into widely varying fabrics, silks are often very dressy and elegant. Find sheer and limp chiffon, sheer and crisp organza, lustrous satin, and textured shantung among many other silk fabric choices.

If it's not made from a crepe-textured fabric, or one that is loosely woven, you may try gently hand washing your silk item, with the caveat that you need to check for dye bleed first. Soak the garment in cool to tepid water with very mild soap or a gentle shampoo, rinse well in cold water, then add a small amount (several tablespoonsful in a five-gallon bucket) of white vinegar to clean water, and rinse again. The vinegar will help revive the silk's luster and pull out any remaining soap. Rinse again to remove the odor of the vinegar, then roll up your item in a clean towel to remove excess liquid. Lay the item flat to start drying and iron the silk piece (using a light press cloth) while it is still slightly damp to help remove wrinkles.

WOOL IS A FIBER obtained from the sheared coats of sheep. It is spun into a yarn that is strong and flexible, an excellent insulator, naturally water repellent but also absorbent. The fibers are crimped and springy, allowing them to bind together when spun. Wool is what makes heavy coat materials like melton and fleece, suit fabrics like gabardine, felt used for hats, light and drapeable challis, and many knits.

Some of wool's related specialty fibers include angora (from the angora rabbit), camel's hair (camel), cashmere (cashmere goat), and mohair (angora goat).

Gently wash unembellished wool knits in cool water and Eucalan, which is a gentle no-rinse wash. Always treat wool gently (so don't wring or twist) when it is wet because it loses some strength in that state. Roll the knit in a clean towel to remove excess moisture and dry flat away from any direct heat after carefully shaping the piece. Woven wool is usually best dry cleaned to avoid shrinkage. Woven wool is very often made into tailored garments with inner structure (shoulder pads, interfacing) and additional fabric (lining) that doesn't respond well to washing, and that does benefit from professional pressing.

Show me a person who has never shrunk a wool sweater and I will show you a person who has never *owned* a wool sweater. Shrink happens, and although it may never return to its original state, you can at least try to reshape a mildly shrunken sweater by giving it a longish (30–60 minute) soak in cool water with a couple of tablespoons of liquid fabric softener or hair conditioner. Drain after washing, but don't rinse. Gently lay the sweater on a towel and carefully reshape it. Keep reshaping as the sweater dries. You might need to repeat the soak and reshaping to reach your goal.

If the sweater refuses to take your many gentle hints, my suggestion is to transform yourself into a diabolical sweater destroyer and hot wash and dry the sweater until it is heavily shrunken and felted. You can then cut it into shapes without it unraveling. Next year's Christmas ornaments?

LINEN IS BOTH the name of a fiber and the name of the finished fabric made from this fiber, which comes from the flax plant. Its natural fiber variations create slubs in the texture. Linen is famous for its use in making garments worn in hot climates—it is exceptionally absorbent and cool. Linen fabric is crisp and smooth when pressed, but can also wrinkle easily.

Dyed linen items can bleed color and unwashed linen can shrink, so those pieces are best washed in cool or cold water, for others you can consider warm water. A very light and delicate linen piece should be treated to a gentle hand wash, other pieces can stand a gentle-cycle machine wash, but, as always, hand washing is easiest on the item. Air dry the garment, and if you are going to iron it, do so while it is still slightly damp. Dry clean any linen garment with built-in structure, such as a tailored suit.

RAYON, made from cellulose, was the first man-made fiber, dating back to the middle of the nineteenth century. It has been in commercial production since the first decade of the twentieth century. The name rayon ("beam of light" in French) was first used in 1924 in the U.S., whereas viscose was used as the name of the most common process for making the fiber, and the cellulosic liquid from which the rayon was made. Viscose was adopted as the name of the fabric in Europe.

During manufacturing, viscose rayon can be blended with any other fiber, and the finished textile can be soft and silky or sturdy and strong. It can have a dull or bright finish and can be silken, linen-like or even wool-like. Rayon's clothing uses range from delicate lingerie to coats.

Do not wash rayon that has a crepe texture, or you will be donating said dress to a stylish little girl! In fact, I'd suggest dry cleaning any textured rayon fabric to avoid shrinkage. Plain weave rayons are, however, usually washable in cool water. Always test for the possibility of dye bleed (instructions coming up soon) before plunging your item into the drink.

ACETATE WAS THE SECOND man-made fiber created from cellulose, patented in 1894. Both acetate and rayon were originally called artificial silk. Acetate was given a grouping separate from rayon by the U.S. Federal Trade Commission in 1953. Acetate is silk's closest competitor for drape and sheen.

I tend to cold wash and drip dry 1970s acetate knit shirts, and other newer items (in accordance with their care tags), and dry clean the acetate fashions so often made as formal wear prior to the '70s. You know those poufy 1950s taffeta and tulle gowns? The taffeta in these dressy confections, usually acetate, is better dry cleaned to keep its crisp structure—the very structure that helps make it so poufy. I have seen washed acetate taffeta that has gone limp and is covered with fine wrinkling, which apparently comes from any heat at all in the washing—acetate is extremely heat sensitive.

NYLON, the first successful synthetic fiber, dates from the 1930s. After women's nylon hosiery was introduced at the 1939 New York World's Fair, it became a raging success—the clamor for nylons (as they came to be called) was so great. Strong, elastic, quick-drying, insect- and rot-resistant, nylon is found in blends with other fibers as well as on its own.

Hand washing (not machine washing) in cool water will definitely help vintage nylon items last as long as possible. Always air dry nylon and avoid any high heat.

POLYESTER IS A SYNTHETIC manufactured fiber that was invented in the '30s, improved in the '40s and finally commercially introduced in the 1950s. Some may think of it as that somewhat-too-common low-end fabric of the 1960s and '70s, but polyester's uses and aesthetic qualities are wide-ranging. It is a strong, washable, and relatively inexpensive fabric—one that is abrasion-, fade-, wrinkle-, insect-, and mold-resistant. It offers these qualities in blends with other fibers. Polyester's most significant drawbacks as a finished fabric are its lack of absorption, its tendency to hold onto oil-based stains, and surface pilling that is difficult to remove.

Hand wash or gently machine wash polyester items. Very often the care tags on polyester garments from the 1970s proudly boast that the item is machine washable and dryable, but you will extend the life of your garments by washing gently and avoiding the dryer altogether. All synthetic man-made materials can shrink, deform, or even melt with heat, so hot dryers, hot water, and hot irons are all unsuitable.

Maybe it's the Virgo in me, but I believe in keeping notes on things that work so that I can—you know the old saying—*lather, rinse, repeat*. Notes on fabrics and what works to clean specific things are easy to forget, but almost as easy to note and save. Examples of what to note:

- The exact measurements of your favorite cashmere sweater, so you can reshape it perfectly (called blocking) while it's still wet.

- What items have bled dye when tested.

- How you got that Sriracha stain out of a washable silk dress.

- What finally removed ancient underarm yellowing from your favorite white vintage blouses.

ACRYLIC, first introduced to the public in the early 1950s, is a synthetic fiber manufactured to be used like wool, either on its own, or in a blend. It can also be manufactured to imitate cotton. Acrylic adds strength to wool blends, and on its own is washable in warm water. As compared to wool, acrylic holds its color and is resilient, but is not as soft and springy as wool, nor as warm when it gets damp.

After washing an acrylic knit in warm water, do not wring or twist it, and allow it to dry flat. Although vintage acrylic sweaters can be washed in the gentle cycle of a washing machine, they are likely to last longer if hand washed. Don't use high heat on acrylic, either for washing or drying. When acrylic is blended with wool, treat the garment as you would wool.

FIBER BLENDS, TRADE NAMES

SOMETHING TO KEEP IN MIND is that even though a fabric is *characteristically* made of a certain natural fiber, it may also be made from a blend of fibers, or a similar manufactured fiber. Let's say you love the quality of silk and want to find a vintage evening skirt made of silk satin. But satin is not necessarily woven of silk, in fact, it is relatively uncommon to find this fabric made of costly 100% silk from a time after the introduction of acetate and rayon. Likewise, tweed is most characteristic in wool, but it can be made of acrylic, cotton, rayon or a blend.

Another thing you may notice is the use of fabric trade names on labels, such as Dacron (polyester) and Orlon (acrylic). Saying a polyester blouse is made of Dacron is like saying an adhesive bandage is a Band-Aid, except in Band-Aid's case, the name (pardon the pun) stuck *hard*.

There is a lot to know about fabrics—this summary is a mere snippet. You can explore fabrics in greater depth by looking through the Vintage Fashion Guild's *Fabric Resource*, which focuses on the fabrics you most often find used for vintage fashions.

THE GENTLE ART AND SEMI-SCIENCE OF HAND WASHING

FIRST, if all that is "dirty" about your garment is a bit of lint, pet hair or dust, you can save yourself and your garment the washing. The ubiquitous tape lint roller is acceptable for sturdy items—maybe even necessary if you have furry friends—but it can pull off beading and other decoration and even tear delicate fabrics. I like having a soft natural bristle garment brush for lighter, more delicate fabrics, and a stiffer one for heavier fabrics.

Now, ready for a hands-on experience with your vintage finery? Roll up your sleeves and let's get started.

Always check for the possibilities of a fabric shrinking or bleeding by moistening a small spot of your garment in an inconspicuous place, using the soap or detergent and water at the temperature in which you plan to wash. Let the liquid sit a moment, then blot the spot with a white towel. Embroidery and other embellishments should be checked too. If cold water doesn't budge the dye, don't assume that warm water won't—always test with what you will be using for your wash water. If you see any color on your white towel, I would recommend dry cleaning. Allow the test spot to dry; you will see puckering if the fabric is inclined to shrink.

Always zip up zippers and fasten hooks to keep these from catching on anything in washing.

Some metal components can rust in wash water, including covered buttons (fabric on the outside, metal on the inside), which you would want to remove before soaking a garment for any length of time.

Be sure to check pockets and turn down sleeves.

The instruction to "wash in cold water" does not mean you should get frostbite in the process; you may use cool water that doesn't make your hands ache. After all, the water you use for soaking will soon be at room temperature, so it might as well start that way. I live where there are four distinct seasons, and in my experience, the best time of year for hand washing is summer; you get both the treat of putting your hands in cool (not freezing!) water, and then line drying clothes in a flash.

There are washing machines that have "hand washing" cycles that may provide a good substitute for true hand washing. If you know your washing machine well, and you have full control over timing, speed, temperature, etc., you may well be able to replicate hand washing. However, the genuine process has the added benefit of allowing you to monitor progress. You can make certain there really is no dye running in the water, and you can check to see if any stains are coming out or need a bit more time to soak.

Hand washing can be done in a clean sink, a bathtub, or a bucket. A white or clear bucket allows you to most easily spot dye bleed and water discoloration.

For every two gallons of water, you'll need just a few drops of detergent or up to a couple of tablespoons depending upon whether your garment is lightly or heavily soiled. If the water discolors with dirt, change it out, adding detergent again, but less for the second round. Repeat until the wash water doesn't discolor. Use a gentle hand while swirling the fabric in the water, as fibers are weaker when wet.

Rinse very thoroughly, until the rinse water is suds-free—completely clear. Never wring or twist wet fabric to dry it, just gently press the water out, then roll in a clean towel to absorb moisture. If the item is sturdy it may be drip dried, but dry your knits and fragile items flat. There are wire nets and screens to help with flat drying, but you can simply use clean towels on a waterproof surface.

Before there were fabrics that combined natural and synthetic fibers, it was a bit easier to decide how to clean a garment with no fabric content tag. If you try a thread burn test and can't figure out what fiber you have, it may well be a blend and that will affect how you treat the fabric. A cotton and polyester blend shirt will be washable but will not take high-heat ironing—but it also won't wrinkle as much as 100% cotton.

THE UNHOLY TRINITY: STAINS, ODORS, AND WRINKLES

Stain removal tips

OLD STAINS are usually not very easy to budge. (Have I said it before? The bit about starting out with vintage in excellent condition? I thought so.)

That said, here is what I can at least conditionally recommend for stains. If you are anything like me, you need to have a few stain removal tricks up your sleeve (perhaps for the spots *on* your sleeve!).

If you have a fresh stain, treat it as quickly as possible. Lift off any of the stain from the surface of the fabric (say with a spoon or butter knife), then blot the stain with a dry cloth. Do not use an iron or a hot dryer on a stain, as you are likely to heat-set the stain and make it difficult or impossible to remove.

Some common stains:

BLEACH
Prevention: Bleached spots obviously cannot be reversed, so be very careful to contain any splashes and spills. With chlorine bleach, it's ALL about prevention. Yes, diluted bleach can be used to remove spots on certain fabrics (mainly sturdy white 100% cotton), but it must be used with caution around almost any other fabric. That said, as a last resort, a permanent fabric pen of the closest possible color might be used to fill in a tiny bleach-lightened spot.

BLOOD AND OTHER PROTEIN STAINS

Prevention: Obviously, blood is not the sort of thing you can often prevent. It's easiest to remove a blood stain when it's still fresh—before it gets a chance to dry. As soon as you can, hold the stain under cold running water, which can sometimes get most of a fresh stain out.

The next step with any sufficiently sturdy washable item is to soak the garment in cold water with an enzyme product, which can be a detergent with enzymes, an oxygen bleach with enzymes, or a pretreatment product. The enzyme protease (found in these products) is very effective at getting out protein stains. Hydrogen peroxide, in the 3% solution that you can find at any drug store, or as the key ingredient in oxygen bleach, is an excellent blood stain remover as well, even working on dried, older stains. Although not usually a problem with any sturdy, washable, and wearable vintage item, delicate washable pieces probably should not be soaked with an enzyme product or hydrogen peroxide. Do your dye bleed test first. If you have any doubts, take the item to your (trustworthy) dry cleaner.

While blood and other protein stains (egg, dairy products, sweat, and urine are also in this category) are relatively easy to remove, they will be permanent if exposed to heat. Don't expose a protein stain to warm water, iron, or dryer or you will set the stain in. In vintage fabric, you will find such heat-set blood stains, and sadly, they are most likely there to stay.

DYE BLEED

Prevention: Check for the possibility of dye bleed before plunging anything into your wash water. Using cold or cool water and hand washing individual items separately are both helpful in preventing fabric dyes from running. Color catchers are sheets that are manufactured to attract and form a chemical bond with loose dyes in wash water. I have found these useful (but not flawless) for machine washing, and even for hand washing.

Once a dye has bled, try using either RIT Dye Fixative (be careful *not* to confuse the fixative with dye *remover*), or a detergent such as Synthrapol. Both these products are designed to bind to loose dyes and remove them from the fabric.

INK

Prevention: Cap your pens before putting them in your bag or pocket; be sure to check pockets before washing or dry cleaning.

Water-based ink stains can be soaked out with liquid laundry detergent. Ballpoint and felt tip pen marks sometimes respond to isopropyl alcohol alone, which you can apply to the stain with a cotton swab. For me, Carbona's ink remover (Stain Devils #3) is a good purchase—it even works on removing old ink marks in leather purses. Amodex Ink & Stain Remover is also frequently recommended. Remember that any liquid spot remover is likely to leave a ring unless you are able to wash the item after treating it.

LIQUID RING MARKS
(WATER, AND LIQUID SPOT REMOVERS)

Prevention: The most frustrating of stains is the one you create while trying to remove a stain. If you are going to use a liquid spot remover and cannot wash the piece afterward, you may well end up with a liquid ring spot around your original stain. Use a liquid spot remover on a textured wool suit or coat between dry cleanings, but go very gingerly (and test on an inconspicuous area first!) before using one on anything else.

Water rings can sometimes be lessened by rewetting the stained area with a damp cloth. Moisten the area enough to obscure the ring. Then use a dry cloth, a blow dryer, or an iron (on the setting appropriate for the fabric) on the edges of the dampened area first. What you are doing is dissipating the edge of the ring, then quickly drying the area so that there is not a new ring. I have been able to use this technique even on dry clean only items. Unfortunately, a liquid ring can sometimes be caused by something like rusty water, leaving a rust stain.

MAKEUP

Prevention: Roll your lipsticked lips in when pulling clothing over your head. Foundation, powder—all these tend to grab onto your neckline. If you are wearing makeup, take care to keep any fabric from touching your face. This takes a little practice but saves a lot of hassle. Another solution is a protector hood, which goes over your head (and don't worry, it's open mesh and still allows you to breathe!). This keeps your hair and makeup from getting mussed, as well as protecting your clothing. You can find these as unused vintage models as well as new.

For new makeup stains, if there is any of the product you can remove from your garment, do so first. Some facial powders can be at least partly removed with a lint roller, while liquid, gel, and cream-type formulas can sometimes be scraped off. Try not to push the stain into the fabric. The two most common makeup stains are those left by lipstick and by foundation. Both usually contain an oil or wax component, and a color component.

The oil/wax can be removable from a washable fabric with an enzyme stain pretreatment or a presoak with detergent containing enzymes. Let the stain remover work for about 15 minutes, then wash the garment in the warmest water that is safe for it. The washing should help take out the color in the stain. I have had success removing older makeup stains with the same methods, although it usually takes more soaking, or repeated treatments.

This said, fire engine red lipstick (so vintage chic!) can be difficult to remove. For such a pigmented stain, try applying a few drops of ammonia or vinegar with detergent in water, tamping it into the fabric with a spoon (the spoon coaxes the solution in gently), then blotting and flushing the stain. You can also try sponging the stain with isopropyl alcohol. A few drops of acetone (tamped, blotted, and flushed) can work to remove that red, but you must be sure you are not applying acetone to acetate as it will dissolve the fabric!

MOLD AND MILDEW

Prevention: Store clothes away from any dampness. If your environment is always humid, keep a dehumidifier closed in the space with your vintage clothing. Allow some breathing room between garments for air to circulate. Often mold and mildew damage in vintage clothing takes the form of tiny holes or staining from the former presence of the mold, even if it is no longer living. Be vigilant against any new mold, as it can do a lot of damage.

Particularly if you have allergies or have significant amounts of mold and mildew to remove, take the clothing outside and brush off as much as you can. Living mold spores can continue to grow, so it's best to let them do so outside of your home! If you have living mold and mildew in washable clothing, you have several options for its removal:

- One-half cup of borax which has been completely dissolved in hot water can be poured into your wash water to kill mold effectively.

- Vinegar is another choice, killing most of the mold species that are likely to be found on clothes. You can soak clothing with half water/half vinegar, then rinse out the vinegar and wash the garment, or use vinegar in your wash water. Vinegar can leave its own odor behind (although it certainly beats the moldy smell it helps remove), so thoroughly wash and rinse.

- Use one cup of hydrogen peroxide 3%, and one teaspoon of oxygen-based bleach to sponge the mold and mildew before thoroughly rinsing and washing.

- You can use diluted chlorine bleach to kill the mold and remove its staining, but only on sturdy white cotton fabric.

Dry cleaning will kill mold, but in the case of vintage mold *stains*, success is certainly not guaranteed. Mold very slowly eats away at fabric, so you may end up with tiny holes even if you can get the mold spores and stains out completely.

OIL AND GREASE

Prevention: Oil-based stains range from ointments to cooking oil to gasoline. Sometimes these are hard to see in fabric and can be set in with heat drying or ironing, so be sure to examine clothing carefully before you wash it. Oil is particularly stubborn in polyester. Try to avoid deep frying while wearing your favorite '60s mod polyester tunic top!

Wash out any new oil stains in warm water with dishwashing liquid (which is designed to pull out grease) or laundry detergent, then wash the garment in the warmest water that is safe for it. Hang the item to dry, and do not use a dryer. Often an oil stain will seem to be gone when the item is still wet, so do not to use an iron or dryer on an oil-stained item until you are positive the stain is out. In some cases you will have to repeat the process. If a stain has an oily or waxy component along with another staining agent (such as coffee with cream or tomato sauce with olive oil) treat the oil stain first.

PERSPIRATION

Prevention: Try using dress shields; avoid antiperspirants with aluminum-based compounds (the aluminum combined with your sweat causes the staining).

A trusted dry cleaner once leaned over the counter and whispered to me—presumably considering it a trade secret—that diluted ammonia is his first choice for soaking sweat-stained washable clothing. Some have success with mild agents such as a baking soda paste (mixed with water) or diluted white vinegar.

My best solution for soaking out not-so-recent sweat stains has been an oxygen-based non-chlorine bleach, or hydrogen peroxide 3%. For me, these actually have worked to remove bleach-set, decades-old, angry yellow underarms stains in white cotton blouses. Specific products for sweat stains did not work better for me and are made of much more hazardous ingredients. Remember, if an oxygen bleach or peroxide seems to work a little, give it more time. Also, all caveats about washing fabric, such as dye bleed testing, should be observed.

RUST

Prevention: Do not use wire hangers. Remove covered buttons before soaking, change out any rusting fasteners. Watch out for rusty pipes dripping on stored clothes. Avoid brushing against rusted surfaces.

You can sometimes win a rust stain battle by sprinkling salt on the stain, squeezing lemon juice on the salt, and then letting the garment sit in the sun to dry. Take care with this method as it can bleach colors out of fabric, but it can also work wonders on unbleached or white fabric.

You can try a commercial rust remover, which usually includes either oxalic or hydrofluoric acid. Rust removers are nasty—toxic, poisonous, and hazardous. Use them with discretion and great care. You must be sure to thoroughly rinse out the rust remover because it will break down the fabric if left in.

Both chlorine bleach and heat will set rust stains.

About dyeing as a solution to an intractable stain: Unless you are really into DIY and don't mind ruining a garment, don't put a lot of stock in the possibility of dyeing your vintage item to solve a stain issue. It doesn't work well or easily without expertise, and you are likely to encounter trouble with the high temperature needed for a dye bath. I don't know how the "just dye it!" mantra came into being, but it is simply not the panacea you might expect from the number of times you hear that recommendation.

WINE, TEA, COFFEE, FRUIT JUICE

Prevention: These are tannic stains, so easy to get while we are out enjoying ourselves in our vintage! Just try not to slosh, and you'll make your life easier.

Appropriately enough, a student in a summer program at the Department of Viticulture and Enology at the University of California, Davis did a test of fresh and dried wine stains in a variety of white fabrics, and the simplest and cheapest stain remover that worked best with many of the fabrics was one made of equal parts hydrogen peroxide 3% and dishwashing liquid. And by Jove, I've been able to use this combination with success—I hope you can too! *Cheers*!

MYSTERY STAINS

If you didn't cause a stain, you can sometimes sleuth out the source of the spot by where it is located and/or its color. Food stains are usually on the front or seat of a garment, perspiration is around the neckline, upper back, and underarms. Grease is often at car door levels, mud on the hem of a long skirt or trouser cuff, bleach spots tend to be around waist level. Rust stains might be inside the shoulders from metal hangers, around steel fasteners, and around covered buttons with the metal rusting through.

Brown stains are usually protein-based, gray stains are often in the oil or grease family. Rust-colored stains can be rust, but also, tea, coffee, or certain cosmetics.

If you still don't know what sort of stain you have, start by soaking any washable garment in cold water for 30 minutes to see if the stain lightens.

Next try working in a prewash stain remover and letting it sit for 15 minutes, then soaking with detergent and water.

If you haven't made any headway, try oxygen bleach and tepid water. Allow the garment to soak for at least four hours, or overnight. I have left stains to soak for as many as four days (changing out the oxygen bleach and water every half day or so), seeing that the stains were improving slowly with time.

Odor removal tips

SWEAT ODORS from way back, storage in musty basements, great-aunt Martha's mothballs, and the fact that just about everyone used to smoke all contribute to the smells you sometimes find in vintage.

In my experience, almost all odors can be removed from vintage clothing except sweat odor on older (pre-1950s) vintage. It can take a very long time to remove the smells of mothballs, cigarette smoke, and mustiness, but these may be removable, with patience.

Again the caveat: Don't start your vintage-wearing career with something that has problems, including odors. Bad smells are often harder to put up with than holes or stains.

Sometimes you will end up with a vintage piece that develops an odor, even though it came to you fine. I know I have worked to eliminate odors that snuck back after some weeks of freshening up. Other times you've brought the odors on yourself (Friends who smoke? Puppy not house-trained?).

It's always good to start with the easiest, cheapest solution if you can: Air and sunlight freshen clothing, and sometimes a good airing is all that's needed to make a mild odor disappear. Of course, if you can wash the garment, that may do the trick.

For most odors (sweat, mildew, smoke, mothballs, someone else's perfume), my number one favorite product is Zero Odor spray. I have even been able to remove 1950s-era and newer vintage sweat odors with this product, and while it starts with a mild tracer scent, it doesn't leave any lingering perfume-y odors behind. The makers are—I assume purposefully—vague about how their product works (it "seeks out and bonds with odor molecules") so I can't say what other products might work similarly. I've not found anything else like it. Before you try Zero Odor on any garment, test a little in an inconspicuous place to be sure it doesn't cause dye bleed or water ring-type staining on your fabric. The same goes for any liquid stain or odor remover. Fabrics will react differently and it's much better to be safe than sorry.

Many swear by using a spritz of undiluted white vinegar or vodka to dissipate odors. Both can kill the bacteria that causes sweat odors, and also mold spores. Vodka (for this grab the cheapest and highest proof) is often recommended over vinegar because—along with evaporating rapidly—it really has no odor after a very short time. Make sure you use this technique only on items that are colorfast and can accept a little moisture. In my own experience, vodka is quite effective for new-ish sweat odors, but even multiple sprayings haven't produced results on older sweat odors.

Closing your offending item in a bag or box with an odor absorber can sometimes work for mothball smells. You can use activated charcoal, kitty litter that contains charcoal, baking soda, or even coffee beans. What I've done is sprinkle some of the odor absorber in the bottom of a garment bag with the garment hanging above, not touching the absorber. One of my experiments produced results on a strong mothball odor over the course of about three months, so patience may be needed.

For smoke from cigarettes or fires, I have successfully had batches of clothing deodorized with ozone treatment, available at some dry cleaners. It can take anywhere from a few hours to a few days, but it does oxidize and destroy smoke odor. I have even had success with this on a collection of Victorian and Edwardian clothing and accessories that had been in a house of chain smokers for decades.

How to get out the wrinkles

LET IT ALL HANG OUT

Start by hanging up your freshly washed clothing to avoid as many wrinkles as possible. Stuck on repeat: Never use wire hangers. They put a lot of strain on the shoulders of your garment and can even rip through delicate fabric, especially when it is wet. Then there is the potential rust... Knits and more delicate items are best dried flat to prevent stretching and other damage.

PRESS ON

For vintage woven cottons and linens, an iron is going to create the crispest detail and smoothest finish. Your iron will have heat settings for various types of fabric, but don't just set and go. Always start a little below the temperature you think you might need and see if it is sufficient. Do a little test on the inside of your fabric in an inconspicuous spot and make sure you aren't seeing any press shine or melting.

As a matter of fact, you might be better off doing all your ironing on the reverse of the vintage garment when possible to protect the surface from any shine. I recommend using a press cloth for most of your iron-able pieces. Some people have an entire wardrobe of different fabric press cloths for protecting various materials while they iron; a basic press cloth is usually a piece of washed cotton muslin.

A water bottle with a very fine spray nozzle is handy for getting a crisp finish when ironing your cotton and linen pieces. If you time it right, you can also work with the items when they are still slightly damp from washing. I wouldn't recommend using starch for anything you don't wear quite often because it can attract insects.

MY MOTHER DOING THE IRONING, CIRCA 1950

Things never to iron: Velvet, leather, vinyl, fur, faux fur, buttons, sequins, braid and other trims, the surface of iron-on transfers, feathers. If the fabric is embossed or crepe-textured, you will flatten its texture with an iron. Go easy on seams, because the heat of the iron combined with the pressure over a seam can create press shine even if most of the fabric is tolerating the heat well.

If you iron something with embellishments, such as a cotton blouse with embroidery, lay a thick towel on your ironing board, and lightly iron on the back side of the fabric, allowing the towel to pad the embroidery or other decoration. This helps keep its dimension. You can use this technique to protect from creating lines and ridges on the surface of fabric when ironing over hems and seams.

FULL STEAM AHEAD

I love my steamer. It is truly the number one most important vintage fashion-care investment I have ever made, and I get sad when I think about the years I spent without one. I do believe I would marry my steamer if it asked me.

OK, so I exaggerate—but not excessively. I have found that a steamer is the best thing for all wool and rayon items that you need to de-wrinkle at home. It doesn't cause any shine, and it fluffs up wool—in fact, it makes wool a bit springier and more lively. Instead of flattening fibers like an iron, steamers relax fibers.

A typical steamer consists of some sort of refillable water vessel that is heated to boiling, a hose that directs steam from the boiling water, and a wand for running over (or under) your garment's surface.

It is usable on almost any fabric, and has only hurt one thing in my experience: Vinyl. I had a coat with faux leather trim, and the outer layer of the faux stuff literally peeled off in the steam. It probably wasn't going to make it anyway, but that did it in. I would also avoid using it on any natural skins (suede, leather, fur) as these can shrink and harden with steam. But with my fabrics, it has a perfect record: No scorching, no press shine, no shrinkage, no melting.

As to how to use the steamer, start by letting it get thoroughly up to temperature. Some models tend to drip on the fabric if they are not thoroughly heated and steaming like mad. You can also absorb drips by pulling a sock over the steamer wand. Hang your garment near the steamer; some steamers even have racks for hanging your clothes. You can either steam on the surface or reach up and inside the garment, letting the weight of the garment help hold the fabric taut. Sweep the wand over the garment, holding the wand directly against the fabric. If you want to steam something like flowers on a hat, you can experiment with shaping it in the steam from the wand. You can also use the steamer to shape a hat veil, brim, or crown.

You can find handheld travel steamers, but for regular home use, I would recommend a compact, personal model such as those made by Jiffy Steamer, the company that invented this most useful household appliance in 1940.

JIFFY EVEN MAKES A STEAMER IN PINK!

One caution: Until you get the hang of using a steamer, it's quite easy to get a steam burn, or, depending upon the steamer, a burn from the wand or hose. You might want to test (quickly touch) to see which parts of the steamer get hot. Steaming inside a garment is a little trickier and more likely to cause a steam burn than steaming on the outside. It takes a little practice to get used to, just as a steam iron does.

DRY CLEANING

YOU MAY THINK that dry cleaning is the gentlest thing you can do for a vintage item, and you may be right, depending upon the dry cleaner and the garment. In the wrong hands, it may be the roughest treatment for your clothes.

Just as in alterations, you can look for recommendations for the best dry cleaners in your area. You might try asking for suggestions at any vintage clothing shops close by. If you know anyone who wears vintage, ask if she has a recommendation. Search online and read reviews. When you find a dry cleaner you'd like to try, take something vintage (not your best dress!) to be cleaned. If you like the work done, try with a few more items. An ideal dry cleaner will pre-spot, wash vintage items in fresh cleaning fluid without crowding them, repeat the cleaning if needed, and press with a knowledge of the original items' characteristics. They will cover or remove rhinestone buttons to protect them from losing their stones. You might ask about each of these things when you bring in your first item to be cleaned. Also, ask about their policy for ruined items. No dry cleaner is flawless, but you shouldn't have to regularly lose your vintage finery because of inept cleaning.

In a small community, there may be slim pickings for dry cleaners. Still, ask questions and let them know you care about how your vintage clothing is handled. Remove rhinestone buttons yourself if they don't. Speak to the manager if you can, instead of a disinterested-seeming counter person. Wherever you are, there is the possibility of finding a really attentive, knowledgeable and interested dry cleaner.

You know those home dry cleaning kits? For better or worse, these add a scent that can mask (but not eliminate) odors. They tend to soften fabric and steam out some wrinkles, but they will never give you great stain removal or a crisp pressing. I wouldn't bother with them.

Dry clean only:

1. Velvet

2. Most garments with inner construction and/or lining, such as coats and suits, dresses with lining, or skirts with an attached slip-like lining layer. For all of these, the lining layer may react differently to washing than the outer layer.

3. Fabrics that tend to shrink such as those with crepe textures

4. Fabrics with dyes that run

5. Fabrics that are embossed with a moiré or other pattern, or with glazing or another special finish that could be washed out

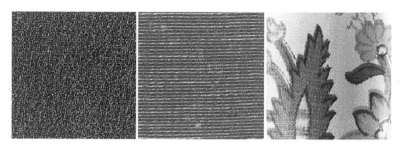

RAYON CREPE, MOIRÉ ACETATE TAFFETA, AND GLAZED COTTON CHINTZ

If there are shoulder pads in a garment, I would not advise washing the item, even if the fabric seems washable, unless you are able to remove the pads and then tack them back in after washing. Their padding can irreversibly clump or flatten; a couple more curses of washed shoulder pads are dye bleed and water rings from the pads' coverings. Don't ask me about my favorite 1940s novelty print dress (with shoulder pads) that I washed, unless you want to see a grown woman cry! At the same time, not all dry cleaners treat shoulder pads well either, so my recommendation is to remove and then re-tack shoulder pads of washable garments, and also find a dry cleaner you can really trust. On the other hand, the foam rubber shoulder pads used in the 1980s can often be washed, and with that era, I'd let the care tag guide you.

SPECIAL CASES

LEATHER, SUEDE, AND FUR GARMENTS should go to a cleaner with expertise in these materials.

Hand-painted and glued embellishments should be approached with caution. You may do as well using cold hand washing as any other way, but first try dabbing each element of the fabric and embellishments with water to check for melting, dye bleed, etc.

Some things belong in the no wash/no clean category, and I can hear it now: *What do you mean no wash/no clean!?* There are items, mostly in the category of delicate antiques, that just can't stand up to any sort of washing. In such cases, it is best to ever so gently vacuum the piece with a screen over your vacuum nozzle. Never wash any item with gelatin sequins, which were made in the 1930s (you can always tell them by the fact that they will get sticky and—yikes!—melt if you get them wet or too warm).

A special place in hell has been reserved for the persons involved in developing a certain laminated fabric with an inner synthetic knit layer that crumbles into powder over time. You find this fabric used mainly in the mid to late 1960s and into the '70s. Many vintage sellers I know call this "devil dust," and it truly is a biohazard making the garment only fit to be disposed of. I have seen important pieces made with this crumbling fabric restored by museums, but it is not practical (or healthy) for most people to deal with. Check for it between the outer layer and the lining of a coat (it sometimes has clumped up inside the hem), and inside dresses, shoes and boots.

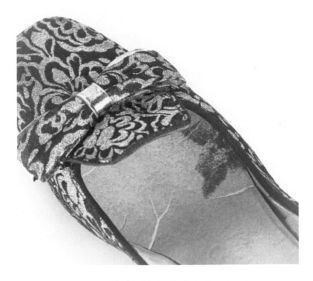

IN THE 1960s AND '70s, LAMINATION WAS ADDED TO GIVE BODY TO FABRICS—BUT 50 YEARS LATER, THESE BONDED FABRICS HAVE COMPLETELY DETERIORATED. WEAR AT YOUR PERIL.
(PHOTO CHRIS MOORE)

MENDING 101

For those who don't know how to sew, or need a refresher, this section is about the most basic sewing skills that you may want to learn to do yourself. Some will take off and fly with sewing, others will grimace at the very idea of threading a needle. For the unwilling, a seamstress can do these tasks for you, but if you are reluctant only because you believe that working on vintage crosses some magical barrier, and that even replacing a button is somehow sacrosanct, know that the skills and tools you need to mend are quite achievable—not museum-only expertise. You can become skillful at taking care of your wardrobe, both new and vintage.

If you are already an accomplished sewist, my best advice when you do your repair work is to consider the way the garment was originally sewn, if it's at all possible. Respect what has been done to the best of your ability and your work will blend in, even if this means (for instance) not using the newest gadgets on a modern sewing machine.

One of the best things about wearing vintage these days is the vast amount of information available online. In researching available texts, websites, and videos about basic mending, I have been bowled over with the quantity of really good information. Especially great for many of us are step-by-step video tutorials. If you prefer a vintage sewing book, I recommend *Mend It! A Complete Guide to Clothes Repair* by Maureen Goldsworthy, 1980. While it's beyond the scope of my book to describe mending techniques in detail, I can help you get started. Once you know a few simple basics and know what your sewing questions are, you'll be able to choose the best online and in-print resources for yourself.

Although it certainly is nice to have a sewing machine, you don't need one to do basic mending. Equip yourself with a sewing kit for hand mending if you don't already have one. Having everything in one place is convenient, and sewing baskets, boxes, and kits can have a wonderful vintage vibe. Choose one you really love to look at and use.

At the minimum, your kit should include:

- Spools of thread in the most common colors (which you will add to as needed to match your mending projects)

- A variety of hand sewing needle sizes (including sharp, fine needles to slip through silk and smooth rayon; you can purchase a ready-made variety pack to get yourself started)

- Small thread-snipping scissors

- A pair of fabric shears that fit your hand well

- A seam ripper

- Sharp pins

- A pin cushion

- A measuring tape

Nice extras to have in your sewing kit include:

- Beeswax to run your thread over to keep it from tangling

- A thimble

- Safety pins

You will want to keep a collection of replacement fasteners including hooks and eyes, and snaps in various sizes. You can scout for vintage sewing items at flea markets and yard sales. These particular items haven't changed significantly in 100 years or more, however, so new will do fine.

Beginner maintenance and mending jobs. Search online or in a book to learn how to:

- Thread a needle, knot the thread, and handle the needle

- Sew a running stitch

- Sew a back stitch

- Sew at least one type of hem stitch

Buttons. Vintage buttons are their own delight, with characteristic shapes and materials associated with different eras. I like to replace missing buttons from my vintage finds with similar vintage buttons. Sometimes that means changing out an entire set if I can't find one close enough, so it is great to have a resource for sets of vintage buttons, whether that is a shop in your town, or an online shop such as Britex Fabrics. There are also some pretty convincing reproduction vintage buttons to be had these days. Look for instructions for sewing on a shirt or flat button (the kind with holes through it), and a shank button (the kind with a hollow protrusion, or loop, on its back).

Buttonholes. Sometimes a buttonhole becomes frayed and needs repair. If you are ready to tackle this intermediate mend, you need to find instructions for the hand-sewn buttonhole stitch.

Hems. There are three basic hem stitches, the whip stitch, the slip stitch, and the catch stitch. All three of these work fine and are inconspicuous on the outside, but if the hem just needs a few stitches, it is nice to use the type of stitch used originally. It's good to blend your mend.

Pills. Those little fluff balls that accumulate on sweaters and fabrics with any nap are pretty easy to remove from wool, but not so easy when the pilling is on a synthetic fabric such as polyester. I keep both a pumice sweater block and sharp safety razor for de-pilling. The sweater block is great for wool and helps with synthetics, but a carefully wielded razor can get the more "sticky" pilling off. There are also fabric shavers with screens that are designed for various types of fabrics.

Pulls. For pulling a snag or snagging a pull, use a Knit Picker. This inexpensive little gadget hooks a snag in a knit with ease, and pulls it to the inside of the fabric.

Seams. If you are sewing by hand, the sturdy and flexible backstitch is the way to go. Search online or in a book of sewing basics for "how to sew the backstitch by hand."

Snaps, hooks and eyes, and hooks and bars. So often these fasteners come loose, or even go missing. Learn to sew them on sturdily by searching how-tos. Keeping spares of various sizes on hand is very useful.

Sweater holes. If they are very small, you can discreetly mend a hole with matching thread, embroidery floss, or yarn. The invisibility of the mended hole will have something to do with the texture of the knit; the more textured the knit, the easier to make your mend inconspicuous. Look for a tutorial on how to mend a small hole in a knit, larger holes demand darning, which is more advanced.

Zippers. Because I'm deep into vintage clothing, I have a large collection of vintage metal zippers for replacing broken ones. Make sure to replace, or have a seamstress replace, a broken vintage zipper with a similar vintage model. If that's not possible (say, because you can't put your hands on a similar enough zipper), a modern zipper is acceptable. This may well not matter to you, but I'd caution you that a zipper of the wrong type can slightly lower the value of a vintage item. Also, and maybe it's just me, but I think there's a good feeling in having the right zipper, even if it's hidden. Using a sewing machine to put in a zipper is not beginning material, but using your trusty backstitch can repair a short stretch of loose stitching along a zipper.

A ZIPPER PULL DERAILED FROM ONE SIDE OF THE TEETH OF A METAL ZIPPER
CAN SOMETIMES BE PUT BACK ON TRACK

A metal zipper missing one tooth is not necessarily ruined. If the zipper still runs smoothly, don't worry about that tooth, it may never need attention.

If a metal zipper pull is "derailed"—slipped off one side of its tracks—you can sometimes get it back on track with a little patience. If it is off because a tooth is missing right near the bottom of the zipper, snip a tiny slit where the tooth is missing. The zipper pull will slip back on track again very quickly from that spot. Then you just need to whipstitch over the bottom of the zipper a tiny bit above the missing tooth/slit, to prevent the pull from derailing again.

A slow or sticky metal zipper can be waxed by running a candle over the teeth (beeswax and soap also work). A stuck vintage zipper can sometimes be budged by pushing on the teeth with a thick needle. You can also carefully dab the stuck section with a cotton swab soaked in WD-40. Once you have it going, launder out the WD-40 if possible, and then lightly wax the zipper with a candle.

Where is any mention of the seemingly simple and convenient mending tape in this discussion? I am not a fan of iron-on solutions for vintage clothing. I've had too much experience trying to deal with the remnants of mending tape adhesive crumbling inside vintage hems, along with iron-on patches that are cracked, worn, or just plain stiff. Also, once a patch or tape is ironed on, you can't go back—you're *stuck* (no pun intended) with it. Go with sewing for a mend that looks, feels, and wears well.

As you advance in your skills, you can try your hand at patching holes and mending tears, discreet mends in lace, and restoring missing beads and trims. You may find that having some sewing know-how deepens a connection to your vintage finds—if nothing else, it extends the life of something you love.

Alternatives to authentic vintage

IF, AFTER READING THE PREVIOUS CHAPTER, you're a little concerned about taking proper care of true vintage but still yearn for a vintage-y look, there is still hope. Or maybe you want something very specific in vintage clothing, something in a size that is not easily found, or something with a certain *je ne sais quoi* that you don't think is available to you in the market. There are two main options available to you: sew (or hire someone to sew) just the right piece, or seek out repro vintage.

If you are a skilled seamstress, you probably already know you can pick out a vintage pattern (or a vintage reproduction pattern by one of the major pattern companies), find a vintage fabric or one that has a vintage vibe, and make your own garment. If you are not able to do this yourself, you might want to find someone who will sew it for you. Your local seamstress may be up to this task, and may also be able to alter the pattern to fit you just right. In addition, you will find seamstresses with Etsy shops who make vintage-style items and can create something to your specifications.

There is a multitude of vintage reproduction and vintage-style clothing websites out there, and I must confess, I have almost no personal experience with them. I had to ask around for others' experiences with makers of new vintage-style clothing, and I got many thoughtful and detailed responses.

'50s-STYLE DRESS AND
HAT BEAUTIFULLY
DESIGNED, MADE
(AND MODELED!) BY
FRANZISKA SCHLUPSKI -
PRETTIE LANES

Some people out-and-out refuse to consider repro vintage while others enthusiastically recommended specific websites. In the section Selected Resources and Further Reading, you'll find a list of some repro vintage websites that seem to meet good standards for quality, style, and fair labor practices.

There are certainly reasons for going with repro vintage and vintage-inspired clothing: You might want to replicate an item that has become unwearable, or something you see in a photo. You might be pining for a pair of 1950s jeans but can't wait for just the right size to come up for sale. You might want to wear something from the Victorian era through the 1920s but recognize that relatively few genuine items of that age are really wearable. Maybe you would like to be able to swing dance like mad without having to worry about ruining a great vintage dress. Or perhaps you'd like to try your own hand at making something your mother might have made.

I am intrigued by repro clothing, and I see many great styles, but I feel torn. If I were to purchase repro, I would want to know that the item is made in a place where the workers are not endangered or underpaid. I can almost certainly guarantee that much of the repro clothing available does not replicate the workmanship and quality that went into the original models, even of day-to-day clothing from the past. That is the rule, not the exception.

If you search the term "vintage dress" online, what comes up first are pages of vintage-*style* or vintage-*inspired* modern clothing. **The term *vintage* properly applies only to items that were made at least twenty years ago.** Is this just semantics, or does it matter? To me, it matters.

Are the new "vintage" dresses on the first page of Google using fewer of our resources? Were they made by fairly paid workers? Will they last? There are better and lesser items that come up in this Google search, but in all cases it is misleading to call modern clothing "vintage."

Try searching "true vintage," "real vintage," or "authentic vintage." It makes an authentic difference.

Finishing touches

I HOPE BY NOW you are ready to get going with vintage fashion. You're probably already thinking about what vintage pieces will work for your lifestyle. You might also be eager to find the right places to wear the vintage you love. For instance, do you have a yen for dressy vintage dresses, but few special occasions?

You might draw inspiration from Kymberli, who has had a prom-themed birthday party for several years. She first wrote to me about one of the items in my shop, saying "I have fallen deeply in love with the pale yellow frothy '50s dress." I soon found out that Kymi has a penchant for the sort of 1950s-vintage dress that you could wear with a tiara. She wore the pale yellow dress for her prom birthday, and has worn such finery to go to movies about princesses. She *creates* reasons to wear her favorite choice in clothing.

COURTESY KYMI AESCHLIMAN

Maybe a prom birthday party isn't for you. Let me offer a few other examples of reasons and places to dress to the nines in vintage. Maybe some of these will resonate with you:

Go to a historic hotel for a drink.

Attend performances where the style of music is vintage.

Dress like you have the leading role in the theater of life.

Host a cocktail party and ask everyone to wear their favorite vintage.

All your less-dressy clothes are dirty.

"Life is a party; dress like it." —*Lilly Pulitzer*

Fancy Friday. Yes, that's a thing at some workplaces. Casual Friday is *so* last millennium.

"It takes nothing to join the crowd. It takes everything to stand alone." —*Hans F. Hansen*

Wear a vintage gown to a historical society gathering: Think museum exhibits, boards, historical preservation groups. The members will love you for it, or at least that is the experience of Leigh Anne, who dresses in vintage finery for events held by the DAR (Daughters of the American Revolution).

You will make people happy—maybe most especially yourself.

Life is too short to wear boring clothes.

You don't have to wear a vintage tiara—but if you really want to, perhaps you should.

WEAR VINTAGE AND MAKE
THE WORLD BRIGHTER

WHEN I STARTED selling vintage clothing I knew right away that I wanted to share what I feel when I wear it. No, it's not about feeling cooler-than-thou or more beautiful than others, nor is it about being part of an exclusive club. It's about expressing one's true self while appreciating quality, saving money, and caring for our planet. I want others to share the joy of wearing what they want. I believe in the power of vintage.

I worry about the present state of new fashion available to most of us, with much of it poorly designed, inadequately made by terribly underpaid workers, and without a sense of freshness in spirit, production, or style. I worry about the use of the world's resources as fast fashion is bought and discarded more rapidly all the time. I worry about people and how this ever-accelerating world makes them think and act.

Even though I have no desire to live in the past, I want to borrow its clothes and learn from its better attributes. I would prefer to think of and cultivate the best characteristics of the older people I have admired—considering quality over quantity, being well groomed, walking straight and tall, smiling. I want to hand write a letter to someone I love on good paper with a good pen, polish my shoes and mend my clothes. As a dear customer and friend put so beautifully, "I want to tilt a clever vintage hat and wear a bright lip."

Could vintage fashion help us care for the planet? Can it help us set a more thoughtful pace? Finding vintage fashion takes time and knowledge but not resources, and it lasts. If you're anything like me, you'll find that the effort of seeking out and learning about vintage, given its unique rewards, is entirely worth it.

I hope this guide has given you the confidence, inspiration, and knowledge to begin on—or continue on—your own path. I hope you can see it is about wearing what makes you feel most true to yourself when you wear it. More than any time in history, style is individual. Go ahead and be that self-assured and stylish pack of one.

Vintage fashion is the creative, high-quality, thoughtful, and beautiful answer to fast fashion. Go forth and wear it well!

Acknowledgements

I HAD CONSIDERABLE GUIDANCE in the early stages of writing from Amy Scott of Nomad Editorial, and from her suggestions the book size swelled—in a good way. My colleagues at the Vintage Fashion Guild have advised, suggested, corrected, encouraged and been the sources of I-don't-know-how-much of the information I set out here. Thoughtful comments on my blog posts, and responses to my questions on social media, have helped shape my perspective on all aspects of vintage wear and care.

Among the readers of my manuscript I want to single out several. Amy Ernst Mayberry gently found things I'd missed, and her big picture comments on the content were invaluable. Marian Posey read the care section and offered insightful and colorful suggestions from her lifetime of experience with vintage. Kym Dahl knew my vibe and made sure I stuck to it, while being profoundly encouraging.

Late on in the writing process, with some ordering issues and a stuck feeling, Corinna Fish came along and cut up my manuscript, putting it back together in a way that unstuck me. Her editing guidance has been the single greatest help I've received, and to her I'm terribly grateful. She's an angel.

Finally, thanks to my husband John, who through his own search for excellence inclines me toward my better self.

Select resources and further reading

THERE ARE A MULTITUDE of books and websites to which you can turn for further understanding and inspiration. For a beginner in the world of vintage, I would suggest having a look at some of these respected books:

Howell, Georgina. In *Vogue: Six Decades of Fashion*. New York: Viking Books, 1975 (along with the 1991 update of this book, In *Vogue: 75 Years of Style*)

The Kyoto Costume Institute. *Fashion: A History from the 18th to the 20th Century*. Cologne: Taschen, 2015.

Langley, Susan. *Vintage Hats & Bonnets 1770–1970: Identification and Values*. 2nd ed. Paducah, KY: Collector Books, 2009.

Marsh, June. *A History of Fashion: New Look to Now*. London: Vivays Publishing Ltd., 2012.

Milbank, Caroline Rennolds. *New York Fashion: The Evolution of American Style*. New York: Harry N. Abrams, 1996.

Seeling, Charlotte. *Fashion: The Century of the Designer*. New York: Konemann, 2000.

Steele, Valerie. *Fifty Years of Fashion: New Look to Now*. New Haven, CT: Yale University Press, 1997.

Walford, Jonathan. *The Seductive Shoe: Four Centuries of Fashion Footwear*. New York: Stewart, Tabori & Chang, 2007.

REPRO VINTAGE

THE ESTHER WILLIAMS SWIMWEAR COLLECTION website is the official fan page for the actress/swimmer, as well as the purveyor of vintage-style swimsuits. I like the classic sheath suit, available in a range of sizes and colors. All the swimsuits are made in the U.S.

Franziska Schlupski designs and makes her Prettie Lanes 1950s-look clothing in Switzerland. The details look very fine.

Another site that was recommended to me was Vivien of Holloway, and a reply to my inquiry confirmed that all the items on the website are made in London.

Heyday! Vintage Style Clothing (the clothes are made in the UK and New Zealand) specializes in styles from the 1930s through '50s.

Because mid-century jeans are so hard to come by, Freddies of Pinewood has made vintage jeans reproduction a specialty. They told me their jeans are made in Turkey, while the rest of their clothing is made in the UK.

I also really like the look of the workmanship that goes into Whirling Turban items, which are made by skilled seamstresses in Bali.

REAL VINTAGE

I SUGGEST YOU KEEP TABS on your favorite online authentic vintage using your own criteria. Some specialize in certain eras, some have a very large shop, some have inspiring styling. You might prefer buying on one selling platform over another.

As a starting point, I can highly recommend all the shops of the seller-members of the Vintage Fashion Guild, which you can search on the VFG website at members.vintagefashionguild.org.

CPSIA information can be obtained
at www.ICGtesting.com
Printed in the USA
LVHW071238111120
671376LV00001B/2